London • Frankfurt am Main • Leipzig • New York

The GCSE Anthology of Music

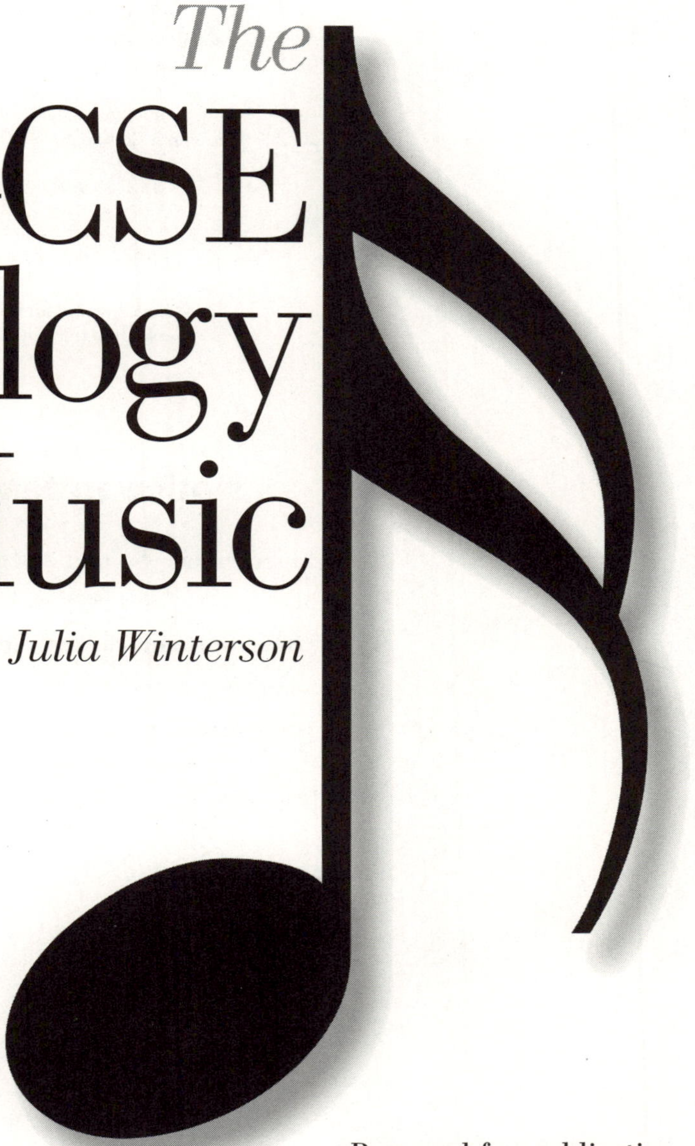

Edited by Julia Winterson

Prepared for publication by Peter Nickol

Peters Edition Limited
Hinrichsen House
10–12 Baches Street
London
N1 6DN

Tel: 020 7553 4000
Fax: 020 7490 4921
email: sales@uk.edition-peters.com
internet: www.edition-peters.com

First published 2002
© 2002 by Hinrichsen Edition, Peters Edition Limited, London

ISBN 1 901507 78 5

Companion 3-CD Set available EP 7599CD
ISBN 1 901507 79 3

A catalogue record for this book is
available from the British Library

Notice to teachers

All rights reserved. No part of this publication may be reproduced, stored in a retrieval system or transmitted in any form or by any means, electronic, mechanical, photocopying, recording or otherwise, without the prior written permission of the publisher.

Design by www.adamhaydesign.com
Text and music originated by Figaro, Launton, OX26 5DG
Printed by Caligraving Limited, Thetford, Norfolk, England
Photograph of LTJ Bukem on p. 103 courtesy of Good Looking Records Limited
Photograph of Cornelius Cardew on p. 80 courtesy of Horace Cardew
Photograph of drummer on p. 117 courtesy of Leon Morris/Redferns
Photograph of Meredith Monk on p. 84 courtesy of Bunko
Photograph of Terry Riley on p. 72 courtesy of Temple Music
Gamelan and drum pictures on pp. 120, 125, 126 drawn by Joy FitzSimmons

Foreword

The GCSE Anthology of Music includes written and recorded examples from each of the topics covered by students following the Edexcel GCSE course.[1] It will also be a useful resource for all GCSE and GCE students, and anyone who wishes to learn more about music. For each piece of music there is a set of questions that cover the full range of ability. The pieces have been grouped according to topic.

There is a variety of easy-to-read scores, tables and diagrams to illustrate the pieces, and each musical example has been transcribed in a format appropriate to the style of music. Although the use of notation is not common practice in some of the musical styles, it was considered important that the scores should be included for the purpose of analysis and to offer opportunities for performance. Many of the scores have accompanying notes to help students with listening and composing. These will be particularly useful in those areas with which some teachers may be less familiar, such as club dance remix and bhangra.

The new GCSE encourages the integration of listening, composing and performing, and the pieces have been chosen with these opportunities in mind. So, for example, in order to demonstrate how a visual image can be a good starting point for a composition, Toby Bricheno's piece *Hyde Park* is accompanied by the photograph that his music was created to illustrate. Similarly, Meredith Monks's 'Wa-lie-oh' may encourage students to use vocal improvisation and experimentation as the basis for creative work.

Two pieces of music are included that use the same ground bass, but were written almost 300 years apart, by Marin Marais and Steve Martland. These provide a useful comparison and demonstrate that a striking contemporary arrangement can be made without using pastiche.

Some of the pieces provide excellent performing opportunities. What better way to learn about minimalism than to perform a piece such as *In C* or *Clapping Music*?

Acknowledgements

The publishers would like to thank all those who contributed their time and expertise to the development of this anthology, in particular Peter Nickol for his technical expertise through the period of preparation for publication and Philip Croydon for his sharp-eyed copy-editing. Our thanks are due to the following for their support and advice: Nicola Grist and Adrian Hooper of Edexcel, Steve Lewis and Barry Russell.

We are grateful to the following for their transcription of scores and the accompanying texts: Toby Bricheno (*Hyde Park*, *Freedom Fighters*, *Real Rock*, *Cosmic Interlude* and the three mixes of *Spellbound*), Andy Channing (*Langiang* and *Jauk Masal*), Martin Clayton (*Rag Brindabani Sarang*), Robin Hagues (*Autumn*, movement III and *Dance of the Reed Flutes*), Damien Harron (*Kundum* and *Nzekele*), Peter Nickol (*WPA Blues*), Peter Owens (*Re-mix* diagram and 'Wa-lie-oh') and Tom Perchard (*Mundian To Bach Ke*).

---

[1] It should be noted that there are no set works for the Edexcel GCSE in Music. The pieces have been selected as representative examples from within each topic.

Area of Study 1: Repetition and Contrast in Western Classical Music
1600–1899

Ground Bass

Henry Purcell	'Here the deities approve' *from* Welcome to all the Pleasures	· 9
Marin Marais	Sonnerie de Ste Geneviève du mont de Paris	· 13
Steve Martland	Re-mix	· 24

Variations

Ludwig van Beethoven	Thirty-three Variations on a Waltz by Diabelli: theme and variations 1–4	· 25
Nicolò Paganini	Twenty-four Caprices, Op. 1: No. 24	· 30

Rondo

Antonio Vivaldi	The Four Seasons: 'Autumn', movement III	· 34
Carl Maria von Weber	Clarinet Quintet in B♭: movement IV	· 40

Ternary Form

George Frideric Handel	'He was despised' *from* Messiah	· 52
Wolfgang Amadeus Mozart	Symphony No. 40 in G minor: movement III	· 56
Pyotr Tchaikovsky	Dance of the Reed Pipes *from* The Nutcracker	· 61

Area of Study 2: New Directions in Western Classical Music
1900 to the present day

Serialism

Anton Webern	Variations for Piano, Op. 27: movement II	· 69
Igor Stravinsky	Fanfare for a New Theatre	· 70

Minimalism

Terry Riley	In C	· 71
Steve Reich	Clapping Music	· 73

Experimental Music

John Cage	Living Room Music: 'Story'	· 74
Cornelius Cardew	Treatise: pages 190–191	· 80
Meredith Monk	'Wa-lie-oh' *from* Songs from the Hill	· 83

Electronic Music

David Bedford	The Song of the White Horse: 'The Blowing Stone'	· 86
Trevor Wishart	Vox 5	· 89
Toby Bricheno	Hyde Park	· 90

Area of Study 3: Popular Song in Context

12-Bar Blues

Casey Bill — WPA Blues · *92*
Bill Thomas — I know you lied · *94*

Reggae

Delroy Washington — Freedom Fighters · *96*
Sound Dimension — Real Rock · *98*

Club Dance Remix

Rae & Christian — Spellbound (Mix 1) featuring Veba (vocals) · *99*
Rae & Christian — Spellbound (Mix 2) remix dub · *101*
Rae & Christian — Spellbound (Mix 3) Old English remix by Andy Madhatter and Si Brad · *102*
LTJ Bukem — Cosmic Interlude · *103*

Songs from Musicals

Lionel Bart — 'Consider Yourself' *from* 'Oliver!' · *104*
John Kander and Fred Ebb — 'Cabaret' *from* Cabaret · *108*

Area of Study 4: Rhythms, Scales and Modes in Music from Around the World

Gamelan Music

Sekehe Gender Bharata Muni — Langiang · *119*
Gong Kebyar, Sebatu — Jauk Masal · *120*

Indian Raga

Shruti Sadolikar Katkar — Rag Durga · *122*
Buddhadev DasGupta — Rag Brindabani Sarang · *123*

African Drumming

Drummers of Ghana — Kundum · *124*
Les Percussions de Guinée — Nzekele · *126*

Music Drawing on Different Cultures

Lou Harrison — Suite for Violin, Piano and Small Orchestra: Second Gamelan · *133*
Panjabi MC — Mundian To Bach Ke · *136*

Questions · *139*
Copyright Acknowledgements · *155*
Index · *156*

AREA OF STUDY 1

Repetition and Contrast in Western Classical Music
1600–1899

Ground Bass
Variations
Rondo
Ternary Form

Area of Study 1: *Ground Bass*
'Here the deities approve'
from Welcome to all the Pleasures

Henry Purcell
(1659–1695)
text: **Christopher Fishburn**

Area of Study 1: *Ground Bass*

Sonnerie de Ste Geneviève du mont de Paris

Marin Marais (1656–1728)

French music of the 17th and 18th centuries often included melodic decorations known as *agréments* (literally 'embellishments'). Sometimes the performer would improvise these; at other times specific ornament signs would be used. The ornament signs in this transcription are those given in the original score. The '×', a French alternative to *t* or *tr*, meant an ordinary trill, starting on the note above. The 'comma' was a shorter form of trill, a 'double mordent', starting on the written note.

The numbered boxes beneath certain bars are an editorial addition, serving to identify passages 'sampled' by Steve Martland in *Re-mix*.

13

Area of Study 1: *Ground Bass*
Re-mix

Steve Martland (b.1959)

Steve Martland has created a 'remix' (see Area of Study 3) of Marin Marais' *Sonnerie*: first, by changing the instrumental sounds (no longer viols and harpsichord, but saxophones, flugelhorn, trombone, electric violin, keyboard, percussion and bass); second, by cutting and repeating the phrases in a new sequence. The diagram below illustrates how bars from Marais' original – identified by numbered blocks below the score – have been reassembled to form a new piece.

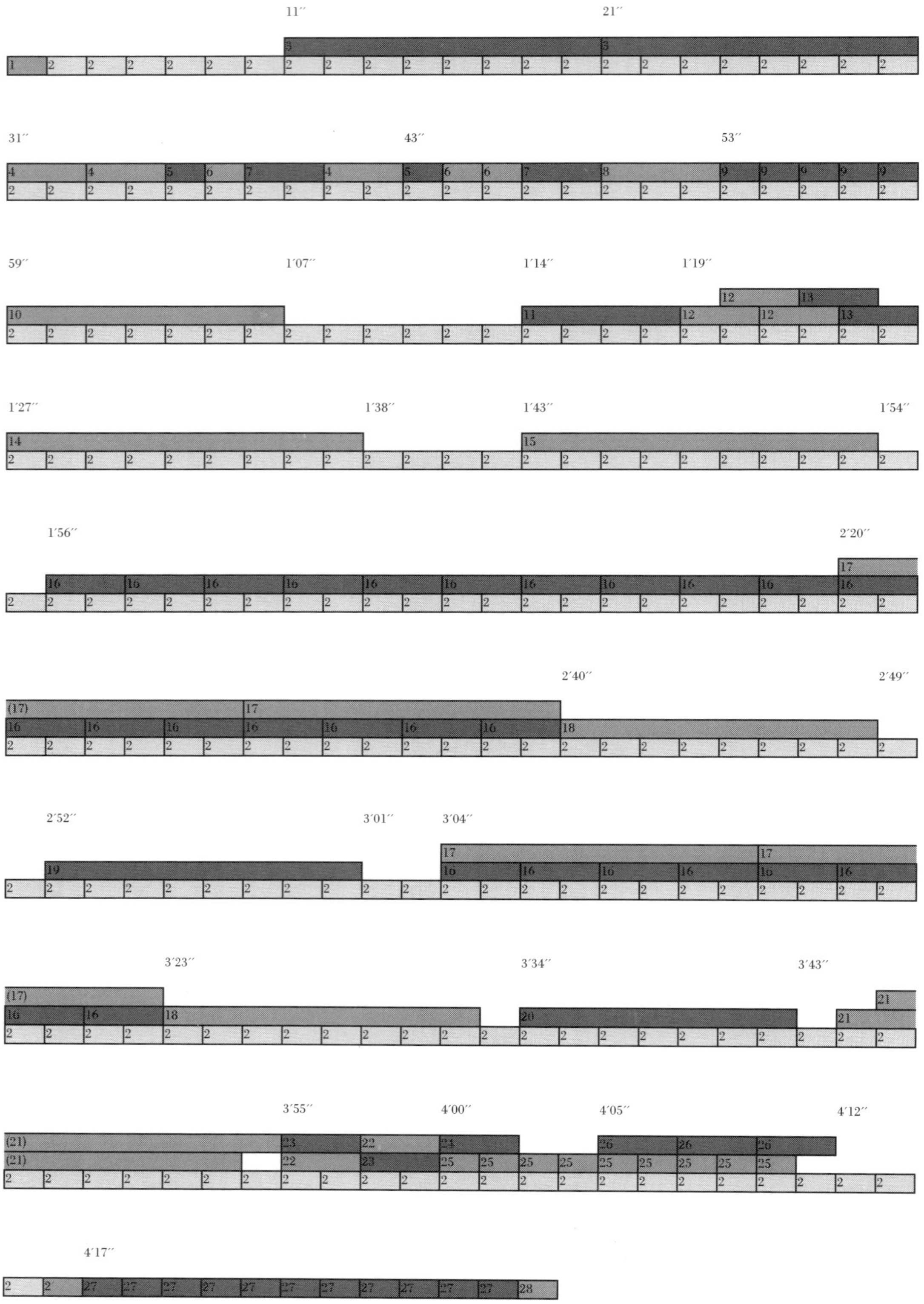

Area of Study 1: *Variations*
Thirty-three Variations on a Waltz by Diabelli: theme and variations 1–4

Ludwig van Beethoven
(1770–1827)

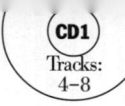

Variation I
Alla Marcia maestoso

Variation II
Poco allegro

p leggiermente

* This repeat is missing in the manuscript and first edition. It is not performed on the accompanying CD

Variation IV
Un poco più vivace

CD1
Tracks:
9–21

Area of Study 1: *Variations*

Twenty-four Caprices, Op. 1: No. 24

Nicolò Paganini
(1782–1840)

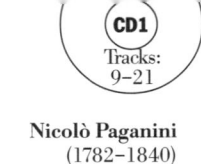

Theme

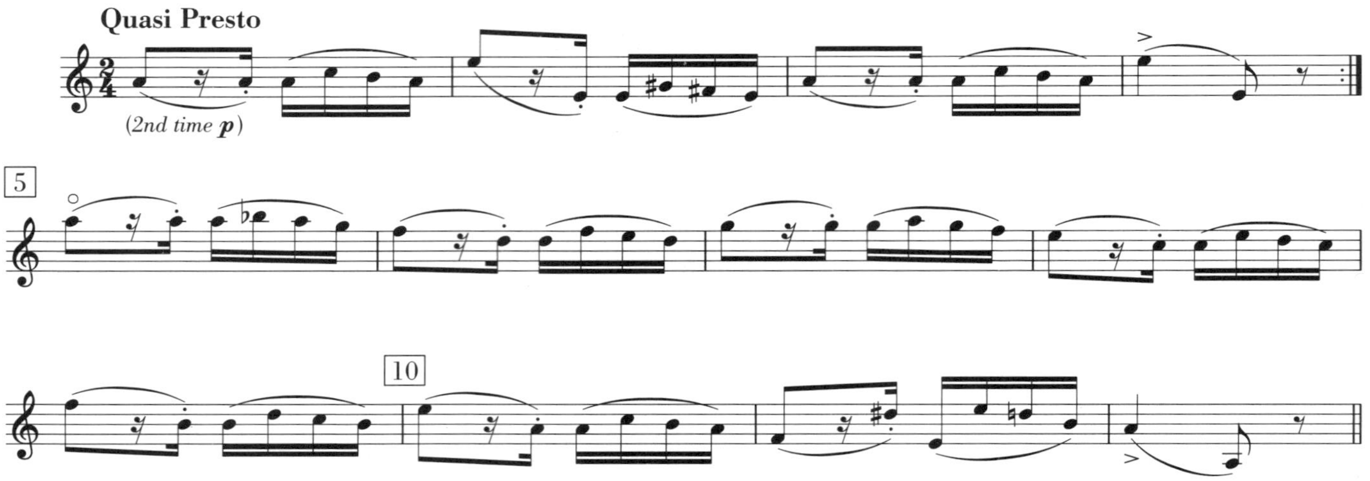
Quasi Presto
(2nd time p)
5
10

Variation I

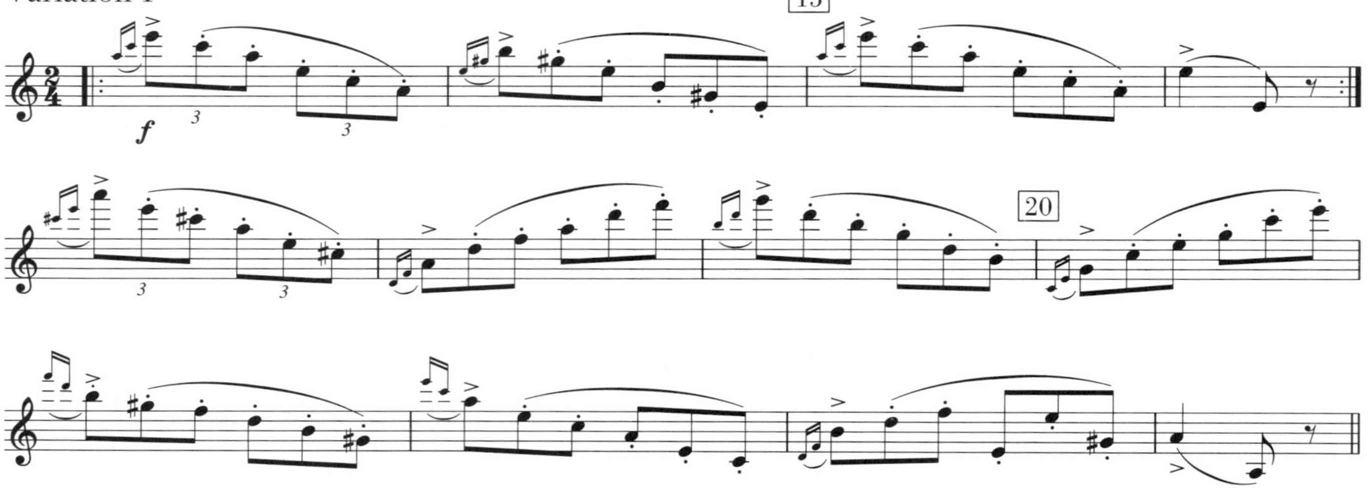
f
15
20

Variation II

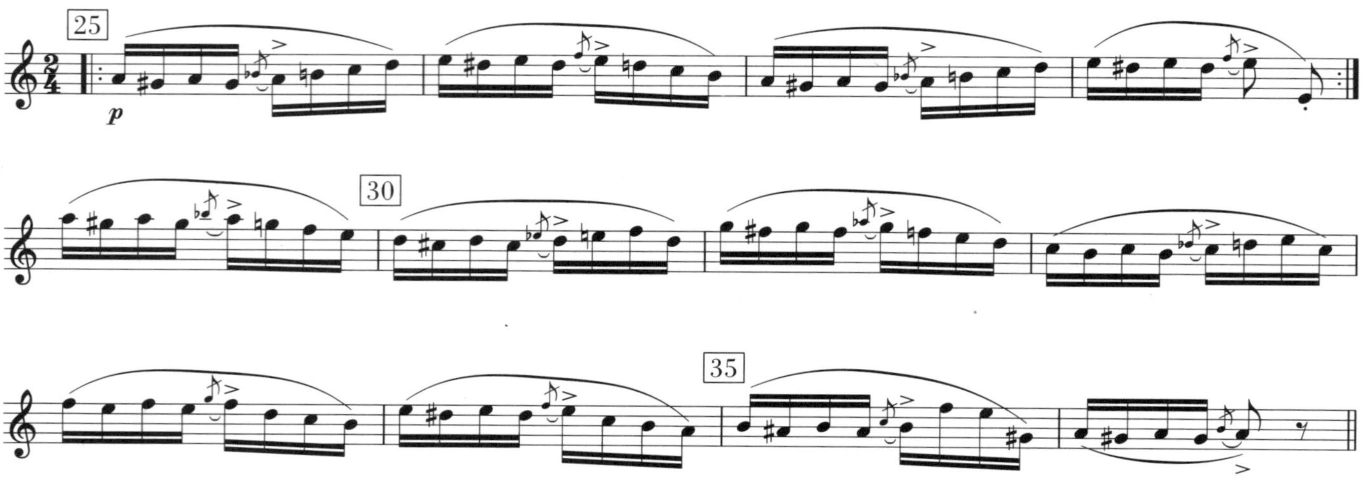
25
p
30
35

Area of Study 1: *Rondo*
The Four Seasons: 'Autumn', movement III

Antonio Vivaldi
(1678–1741)

I cacciator alla nov' alba à caccia Con corni, Schioppi, e cani escono fuore/
The hunters at earliest dawn go out to hunt with horns, shotguns and hounds;

La caccia/*The hunt*

Allegro

Solo violin, Strings and Basso continuo

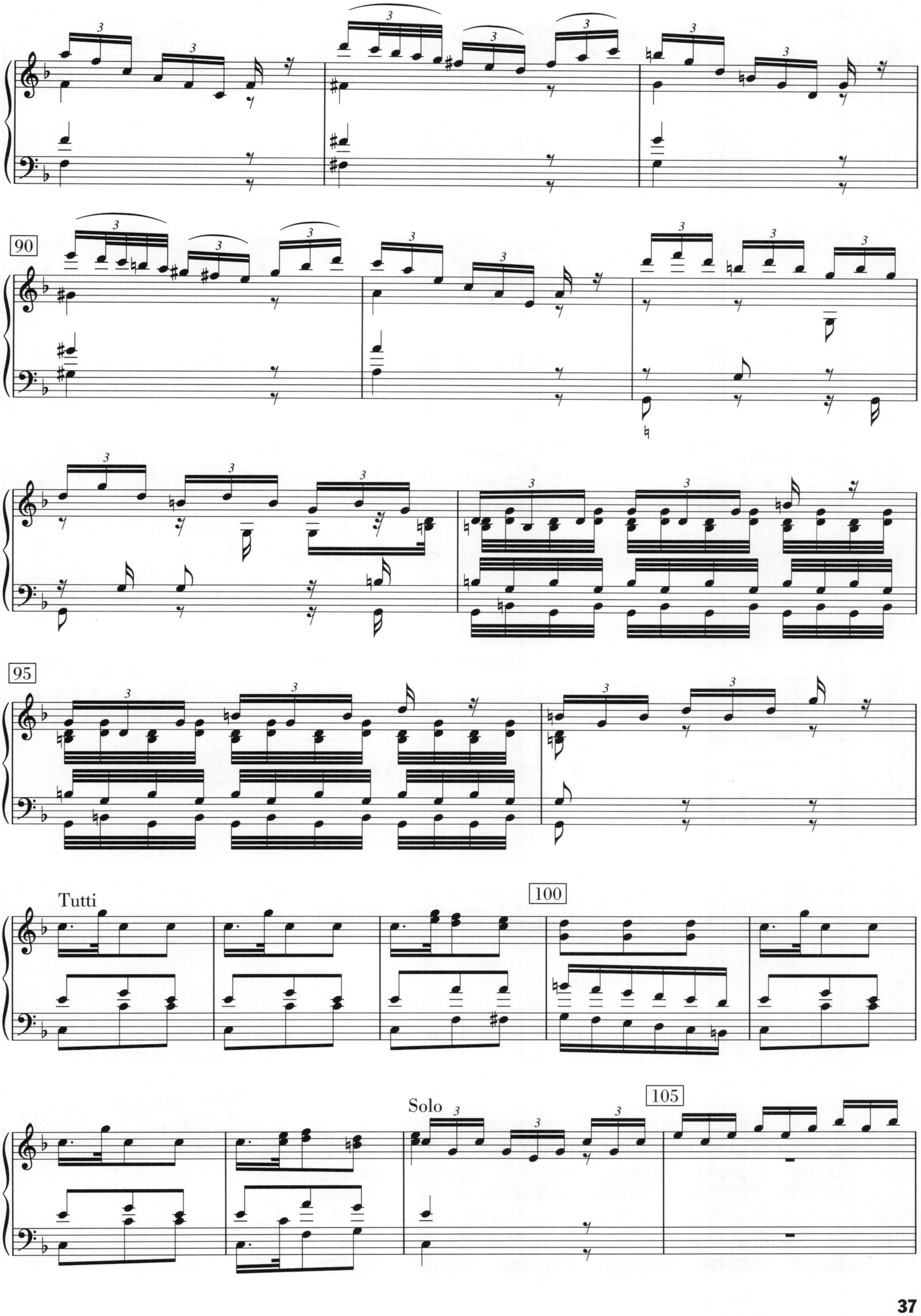
90
95
Tutti
100
Solo
105

Languida di fuggir, mà oppressa muore/
tired of flight, but quite overcome, it dies.
*La Fiera fuggendo Muore/The fleeing wild
beast dies*

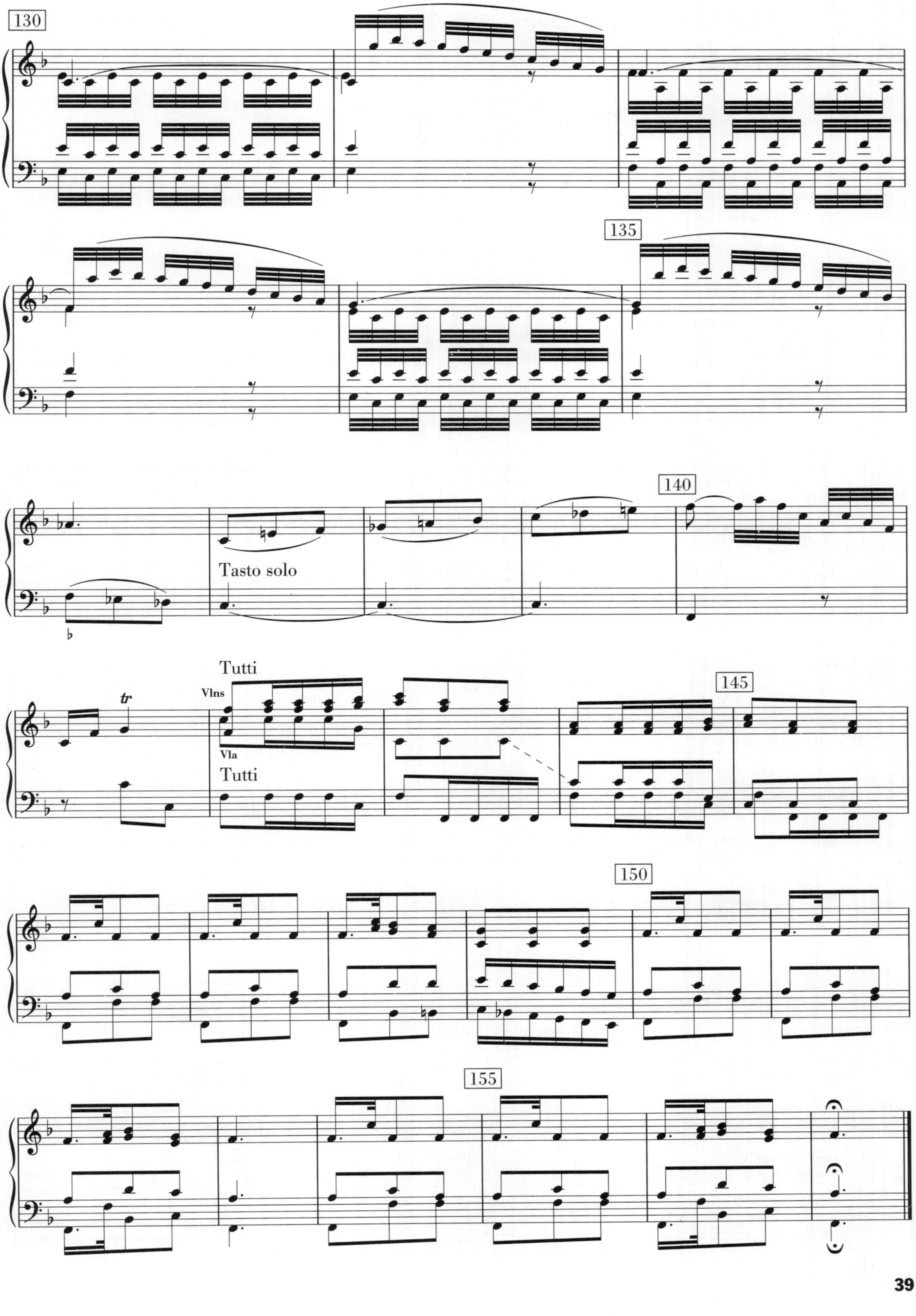
130
135
140
Tasto solo
Tutti
Vlns
Vla
Tutti
145
150
155

Area of Study 1: *Rondo*
Clarinet Quintet in B♭: movement IV

Carl Maria von Weber (1786–1826)

The following plan shows how Weber alternates the main theme (A) with contrasting episodes (B, C and D) for the first part of this rondo. Later in the movement the structure is less clearly defined, as Weber develops the thematic material by presenting it in new ways, re-scoring it and using different keys, for example.

Bars: 1-10	11-23	24-31	32-68	69-106	106-120	121-128	129-141	142-149
A	B	A	C	D	A¹	A	B	A

41

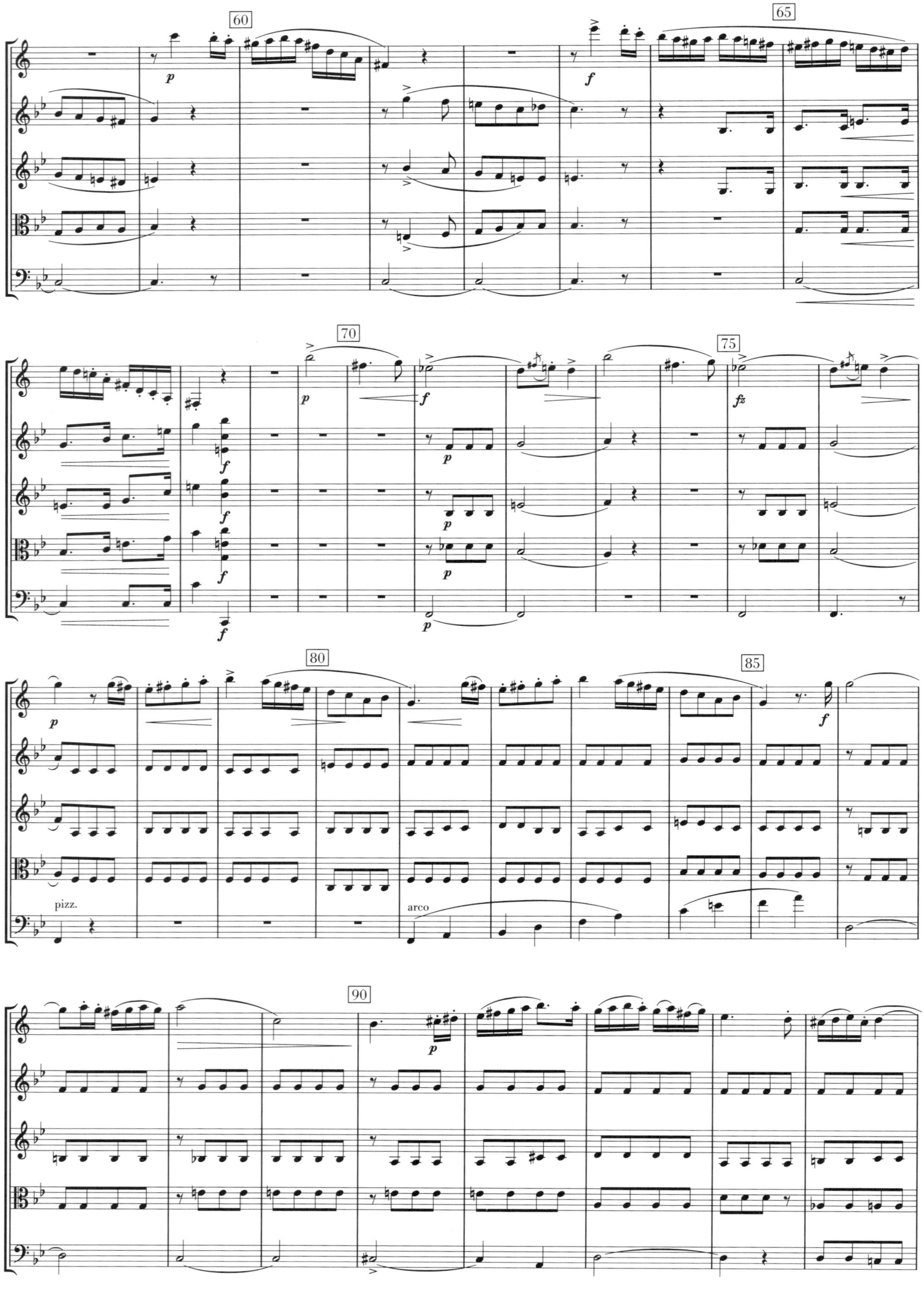
60
65
70
75
80
85
90
p
f
fz
pizz.
arco

43

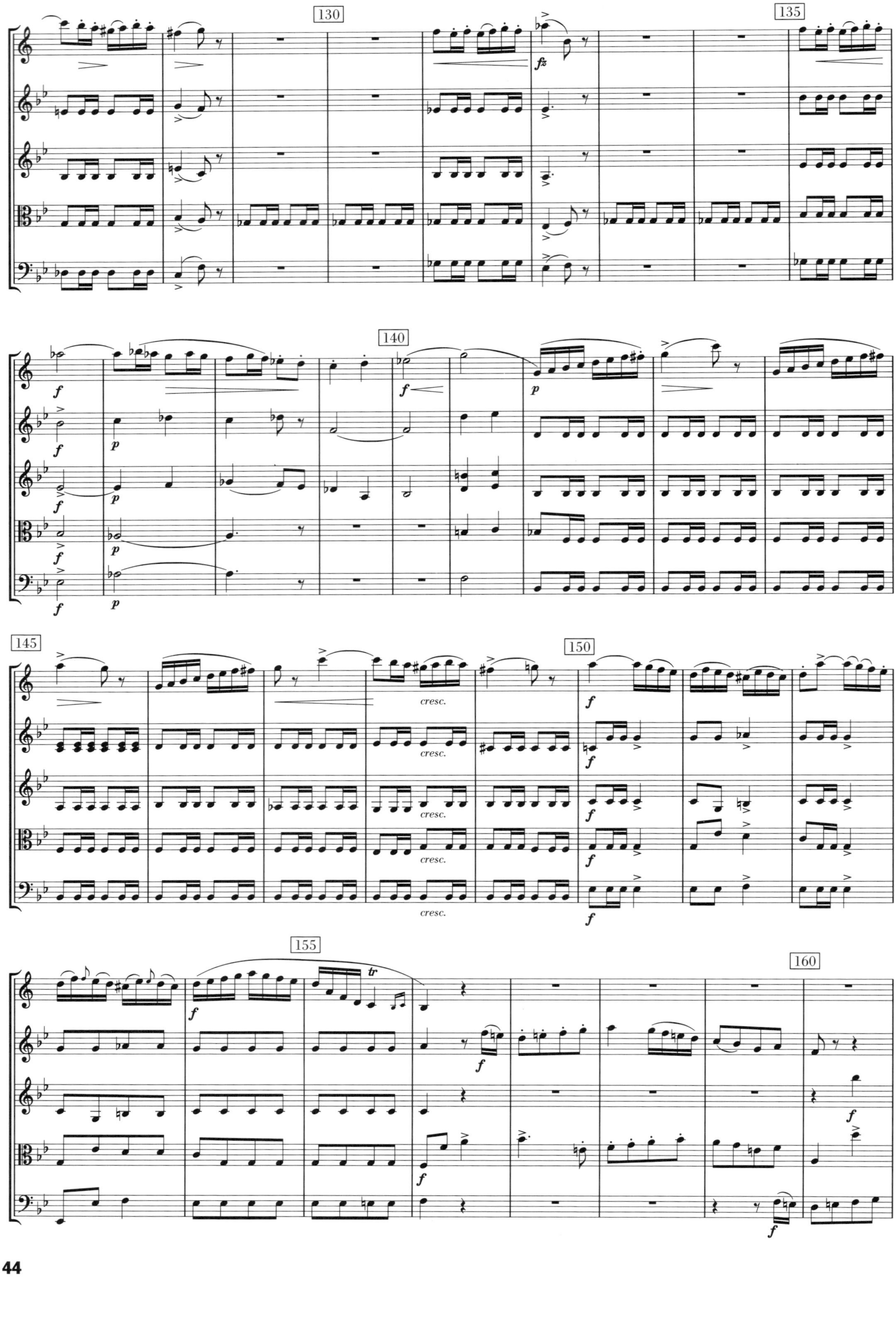
130
135
140
145
150
cresc.
155
160

45

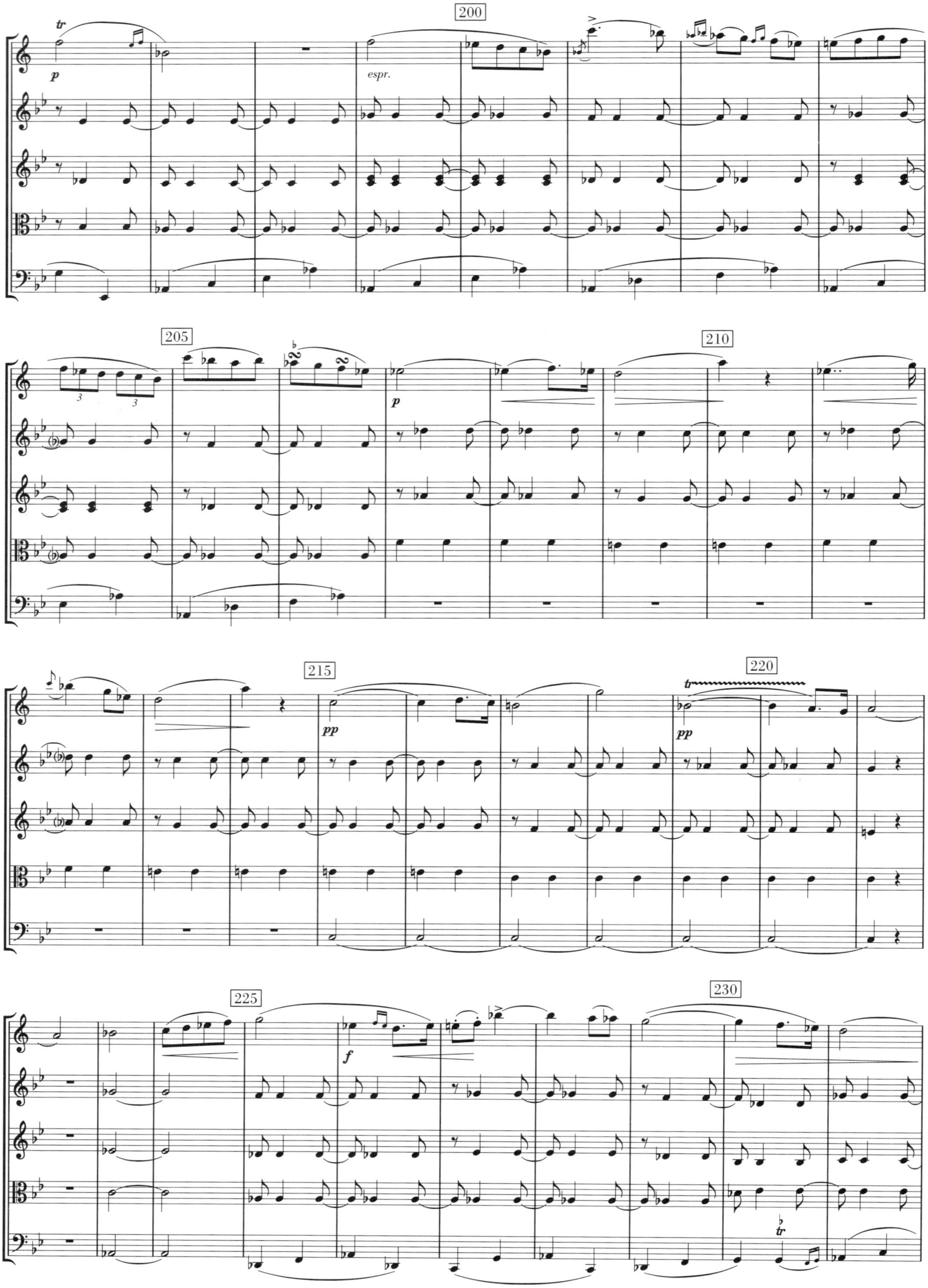
200
espr.
205
210
215
pp
220
225
f
230

47

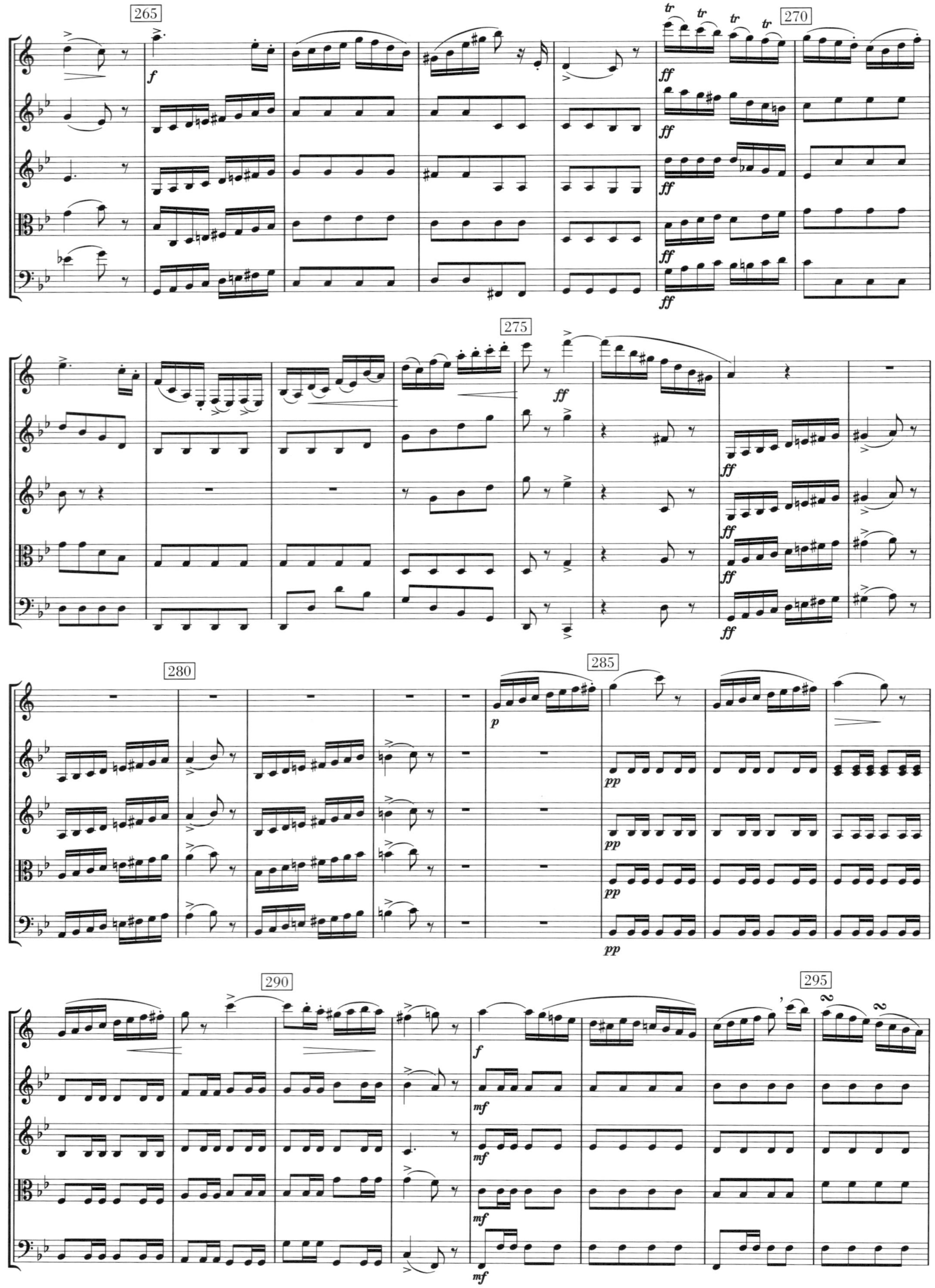
265
270
tr
f
ff
275
ff
280
285
p
pp
290
295
mf

49

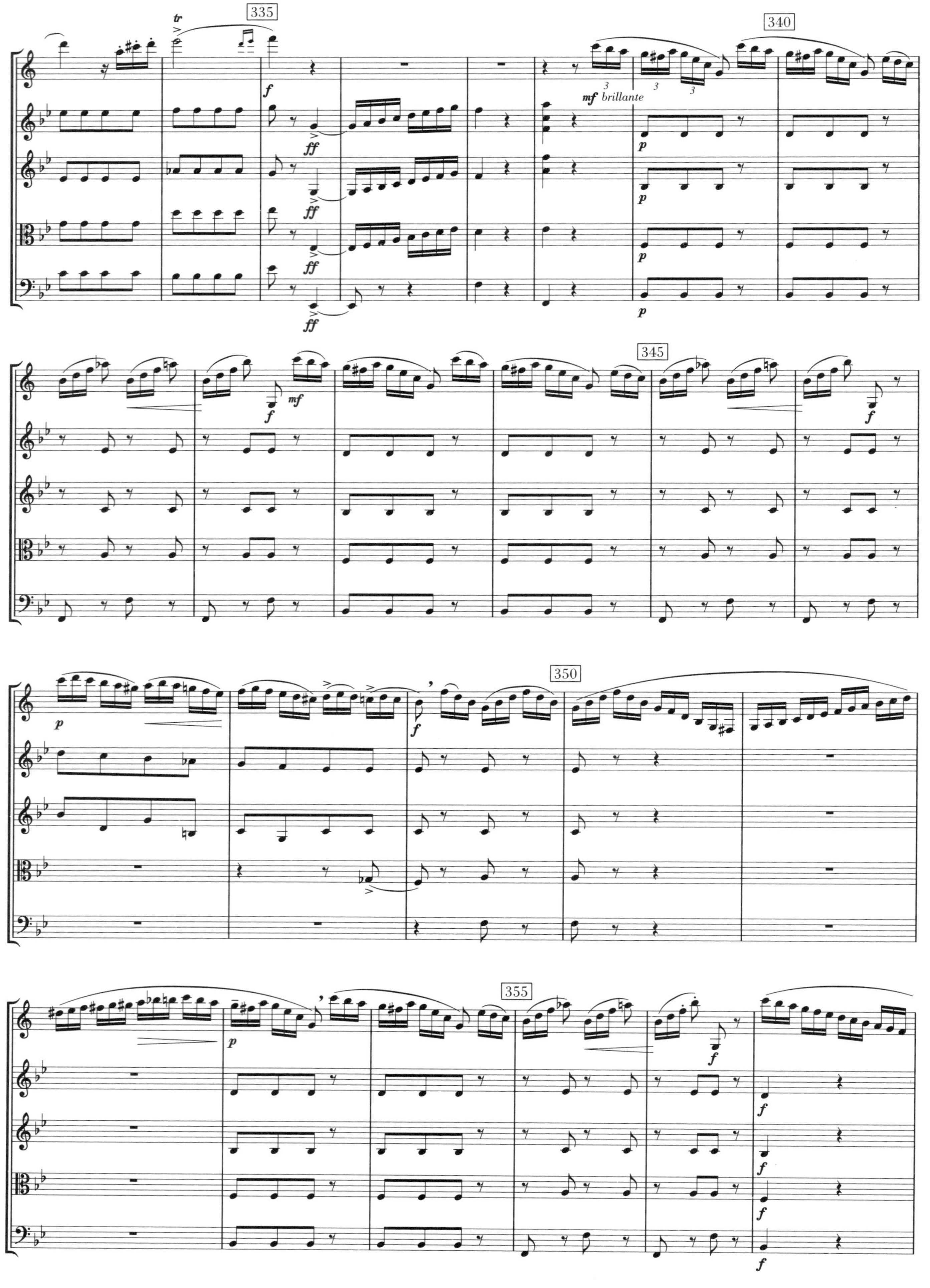
335
340
mf brillante
345
350
355

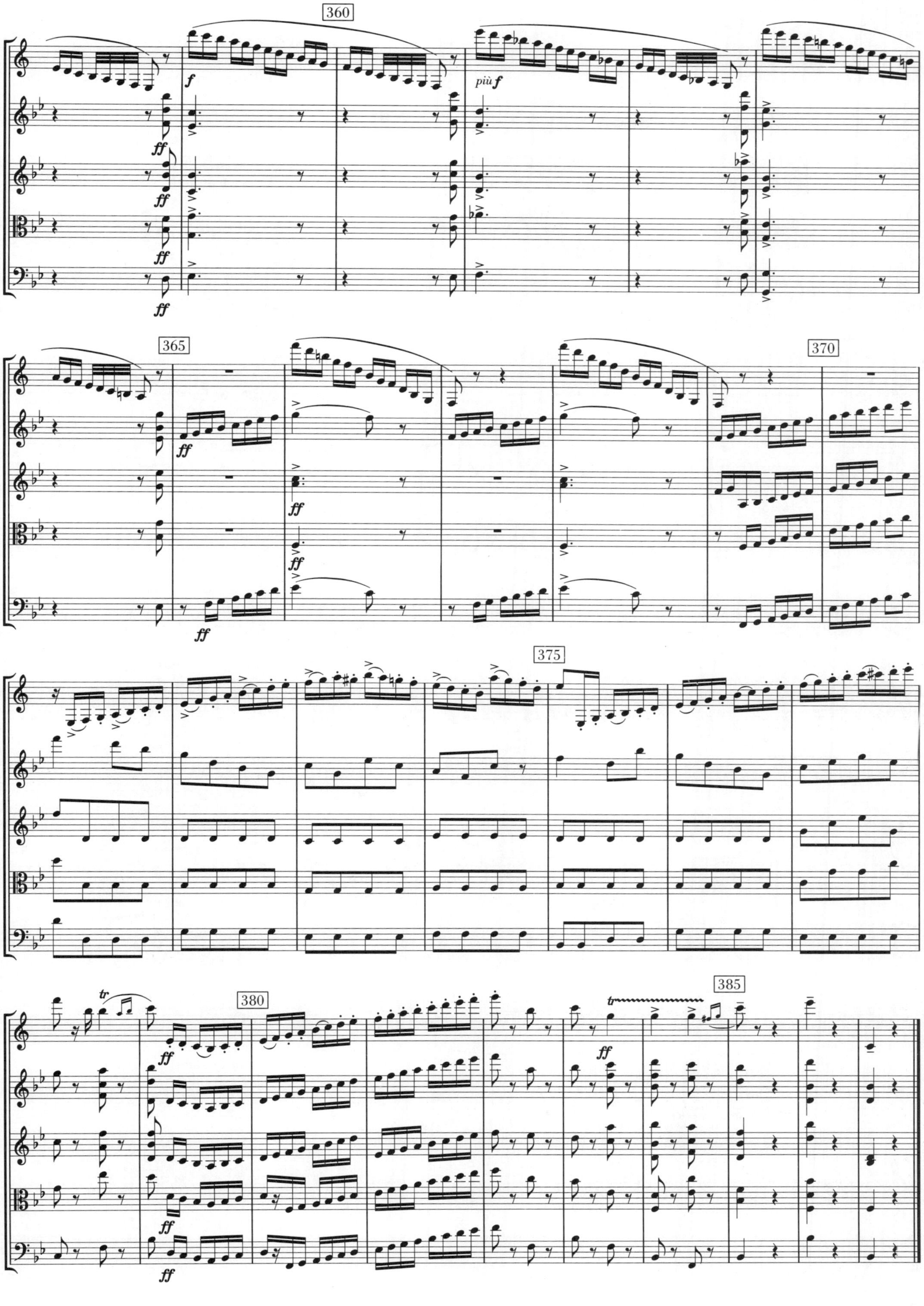
360
f
più f
ff
365
370
375
380
385
tr

Area of Study 1: *Ternary Form*

'He was despised'
from Messiah

George Frideric Handel
(1685–1759)

25
He was des-pi-sed, re-ject-ed,
tr
p
He was des - pi - sed and re-ject - ed of men, a man of sor-rows and ac - quaint-ed with
30
grief, a man of sor-rows, and ac - quaint - ed with grief, He was des - pi - sed,
tr
p
35
re-ject-ed, a man of sor-rows, and ac-quaint - ed with grief, and ac-quaint - ed with
tr
40
[ad lib.]
[a tempo]
grief, a man of sor-rows, and ac-quaint - ed with grief.
tr
f

45
tr
p
f
Fine
50
He gave His back to the smi - ters,
un poco p
He gave His back to the smi - ters, and His cheeks to
them that pluck - ed off the hair, and His cheeks to
55

them that pluck-ed off the hair, and His cheeks to them that pluck-ed off the hair: He hid not His face from shame and spit-ting, He hid not His face from shame, from shame, He hid not His face from shame, from shame and spit-ting.

D. C. al Fine

Area of Study 1: *Ternary Form*
Symphony No. 40 in G minor: movement III

Wolfgang Amadeus Mozart
(1756–1791)

57

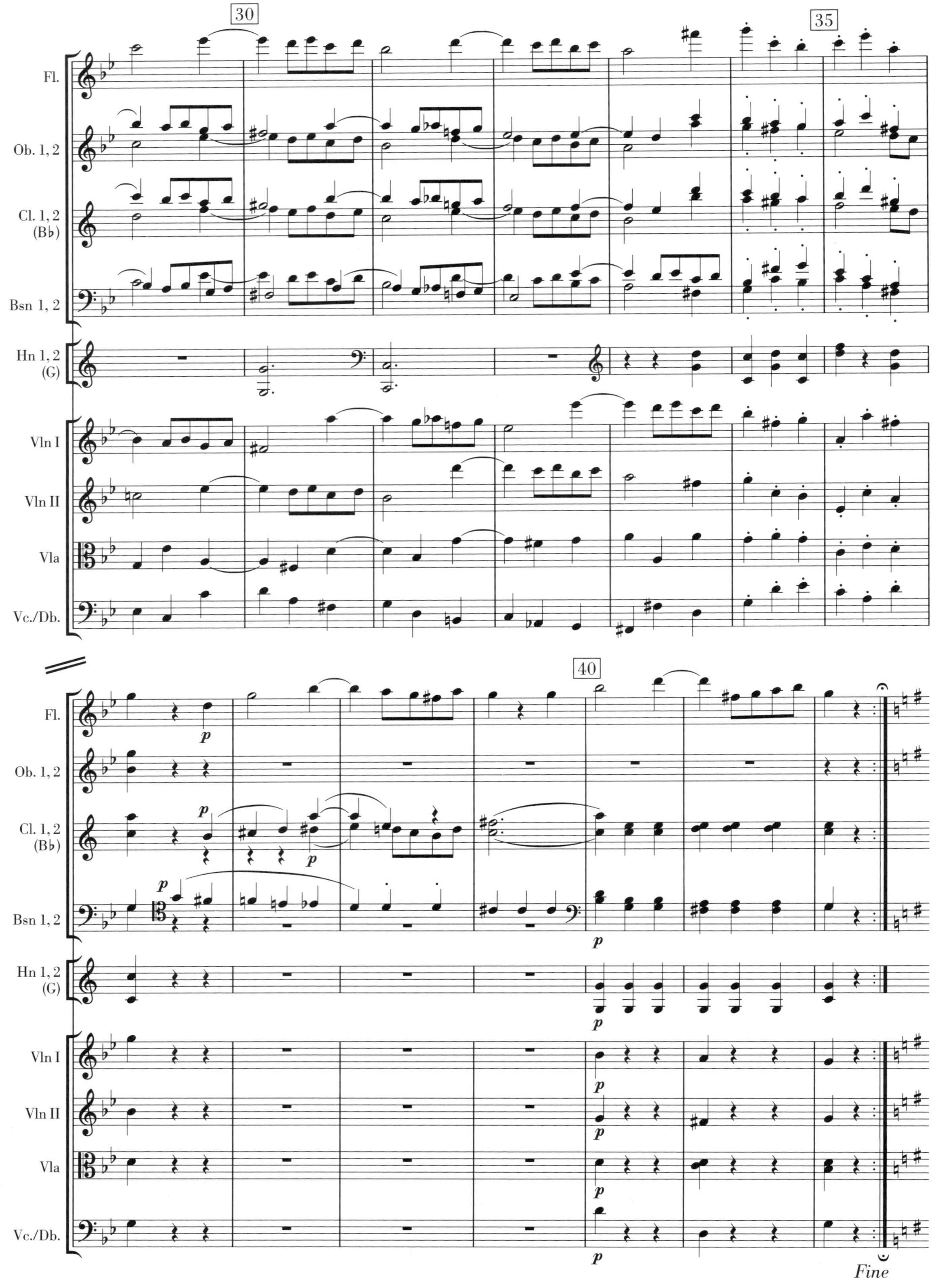
30
35
Fl.
Ob. 1, 2
Cl. 1, 2 (B♭)
Bsn 1, 2
Hn 1, 2 (G)
Vln I
Vln II
Vla
Vc./Db.
40
p
Fine

Trio

D.C. Menuetto

Area of Study 1: *Ternary Form*
Dance of the Reed Pipes *from* The Nutcracker

Pyotr Tchaikovsky
(1840–1893)

This is a reduction of the full score. As well as the usual strings (first and second violins, violas, cellos and double basses) Tchaikovsky uses an augmented woodwind section (3 flutes, 2 oboes, a cor anglais, 2 clarinets in A, a bass clarinet and two bassoons) and brass (4 French horns, 2 trumpets in A, 2 tenor trombones, a bass trombone and a tuba). The percussion section features cymbals and timpani.

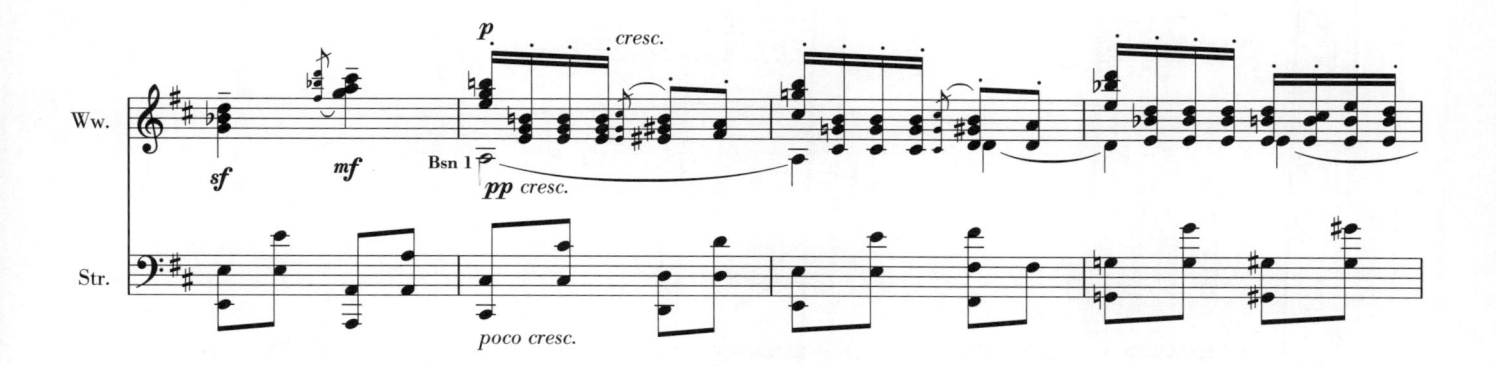

20
(Fls)
Ww.
ff
C.A.
f
espress.
Str.
mf
p
B. Cl.
25
Vlns
pizz.
arco
Vla, Vc. e Db.
Vlns, Vla (arco)
Vc. e Db.
sempre p
30
sf
poco più f

(Fls)
Ww.
p
cresc.
(Vlns, Vla)
Str.
(Vc. e Db.)
pizz.
cresc.
cresc.
f
35
p
Ww./
Brass
Hn 1, 2
mf
p
(Fls)
mf
mf
p
mf
sempre p
Ww.
sf
mf
p cresc.
poco più f
p
cresc.
cresc.
40
(Fls)
Ww./
Brass
f
Obs, C.A.,
Cl. 1, Hns
f
Cls
Tpts
p
pizz.
f
+ Bsns, B. Cl.
f

(Tpts)
Brass
p
Hns, Tbns
Tbn 3, Tuba
p
Cym.
p
Perc.
Timp.
pp
45
50
(Tpts)
Vlns arco
+ C.A., Cls
+ B. Cl., Bsns, Vc. e Db.
Full Orch.
sempre spiccato

55
Full Orch.
Perc.
60
Fls
p
Full Orch.
Vln II, Vla
pizz.
p
Vc. e Db.
pizz.
p
Perc.
Ww.
mf
Vlns, I/II
pizz.
p
Vlns, Vla arco
p
Str.
Vc. e Db.
pizz.
sempre p
65
Ww.
sf
mf
p
Str.
poco più f
p

66

AREA OF STUDY

2

New Directions in Western Classical Music

1900 to the present day

Serialism
Minimalism
Experimental Music
Electronic Music

Area of Study 2: *Serialism*
Variations for Piano, Op. 27: movement II

Anton Webern (1883–1945)

Area of Study 2: *Serialism*
Fanfare for a New Theatre

Igor Stravinsky
(1882–1971)

Area of Study 2: *Minimalism*
In C

Terry Riley (b. 1935)

The composer's performance directions are given overleaf

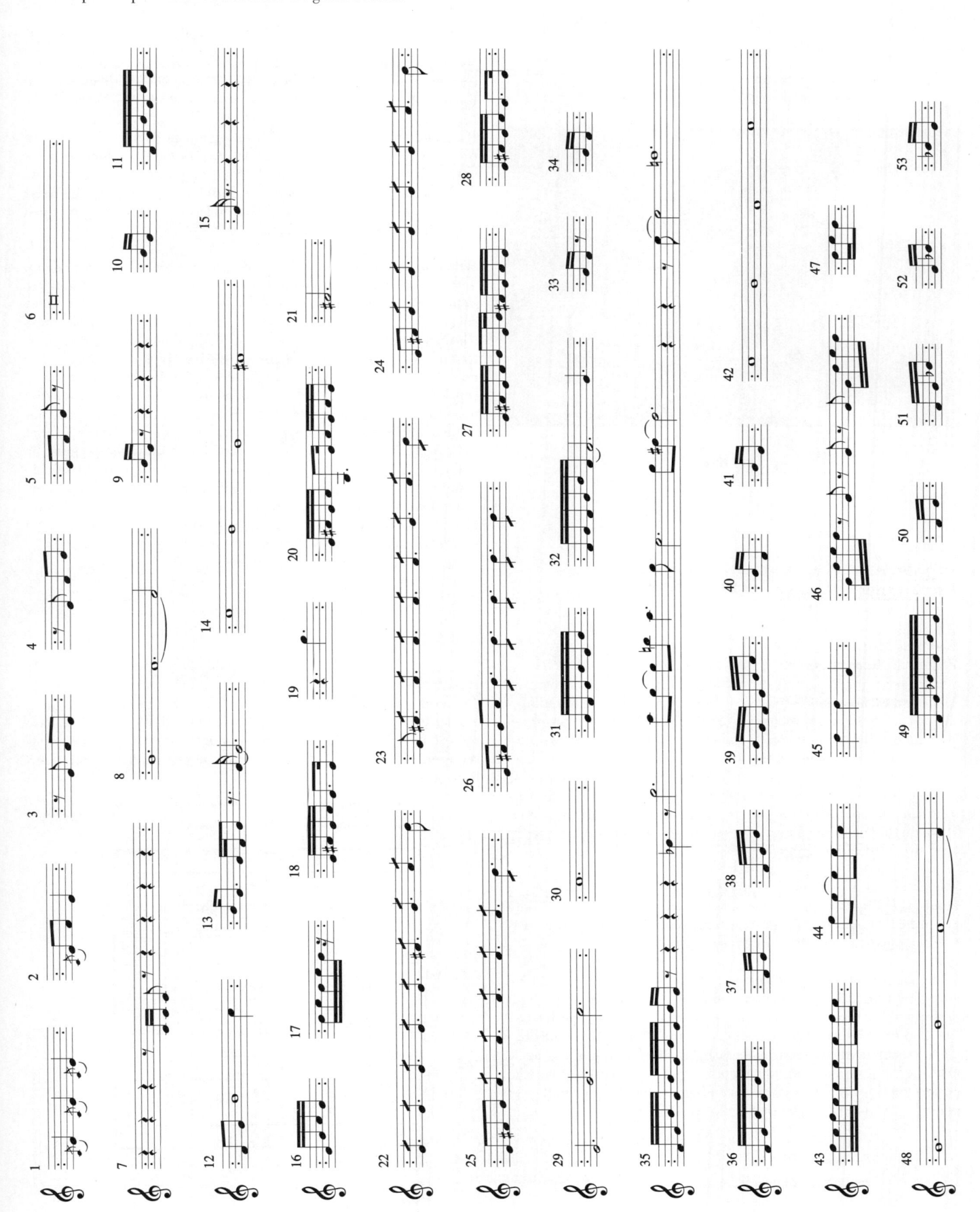

Terry Riley

In C
Performance directions

The 53 repeating patterns are to be played in consecutive order starting with 1 and ending on 53.

All performers play from the same part except the 'pulse'.

When possible all parts are to be played in the octave written. Octave transpositions, especially downwards, must be done with attention to the overall balance.

If needed or desired, a steady quaver (eighth-note) pulse is played on the top octaves of a piano, marimba or vibraphone to help keep the ensemble together rhythmically. During the course of the performance the pulse may be traded off between players. The pulse is stated before the rest of the ensemble enters and is maintained throughout the duration of the work.

When beginning, each performer decides for himself when to enter. A strong unison feeling should be established for 5 or 10 minutes before different alignments of the patterns are attempted. The most successful performances are those in which the ensemble stays within a compass of four or five patterns. Although each performer is free to move from figure to figure at his own rate, it is important to note that steady continuous repetition will stabilize his part so that it can be related to by other performers and he, in turn, can make a meaningful relationship to them. Above all, performers must not wander ahead or lag behind the nucleus of the ensemble so that their part is removed from context, and an absolute tempo must be maintained. During the course of the composition the ensemble should attempt to regroup occasionally in a strong unison pattern. Individual patterns, when started on different parts of the measure may play against themselves canonically with a quaver (eighth-note) separation generally being the smallest effective point of imitation.

Terry Riley

Clapping Music
Performance directions

The number of repeats is fixed at 12 repeats per bar. The duration of the piece should be approximately 5 minutes. The second performer should keep his or her downbeat where it is written, on the first beat of each measure and not on the first beat of the group of three claps, so that the downbeat always falls on a new beat of the unchanging pattern. No other accents should be made. It is for this reason that a time signature of 6/4 or 12/8 is not given – to avoid metrical accents. To begin the piece one player may set the tempo by counting quietly; 'one, two, three, four, five, six'.

The choice of a particular clapping sound, i.e. with cupped or flat hands, is left up to the performers. Whichever timbre is chosen, both performers should try and get the same one so that their two parts will blend to produce one overall resulting pattern.

In a hall holding 200 people or more the clapping should be amplified with either a single omni-directional microphone for both performers, or two directional microphones; one for each performer. In either case the amplification should be mixed into mono and both parts fed equally to all loudspeakers. In smaller live rooms the piece may be performed without amplification. In either case the performers should perform while standing as close to one another as possible so as to hear each other well.

Steve Reich

The grid score below shows another way of representing Clapping Music. It is read from left to right and top to bottom. Each square represents a beat – the dots represent claps and the blank squares represent silent beats. Notice how in this score the phase shifting can be seen clearly.

Area of Study 2: *Minimalism*
Clapping Music

Steve Reich (b. 1936)

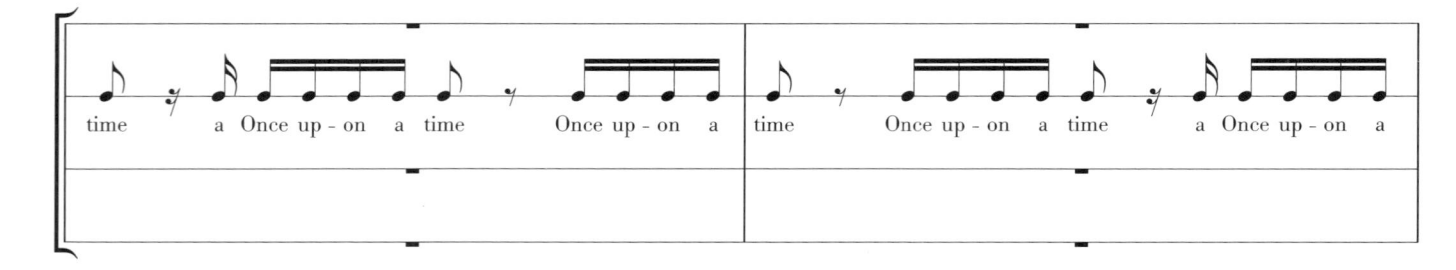

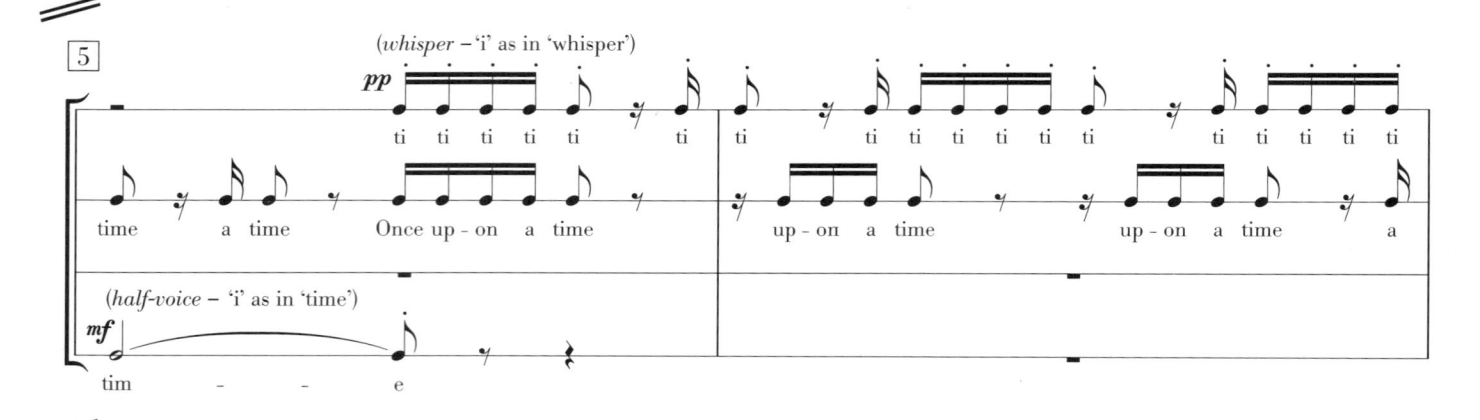

Area of Study 2: *Experimental Music*
Living Room Music: 'Story'

John Cage
(1912–1992)
text: **Gertrude Stein**

Story is the second movement of *Living Room Music* for percussion and speech quartet. The other three movements are all for percussion quartet. Cage directs performers to use 'any household objects or architectural elements' as instruments for these movements. His suggestions include magazines, newspapers, largish books, tables, floors and doors. In *Story*, however, the performers use only vocal sounds.

10
ti ti ti ti ti ti ti ti ti
world world
On - ce On - ce
ti ti ti ti ti ti ti ti ti ti ti ti
worl - d worl - d
On - ce On - ce On - ce
ti ti ti ti ti ti ti ti ti ti ti
worl - d worl - d
On - ce On - ce
ti ti ti ti ti ti
Once up - on a time a time up - on a time a time up - on a time a time a
On - ce On - ce On - ce On - ce On - ce
mf
tim - e
p
(whistle)
(half-voice)
pp
15
the world was roun - d
Once up - on a time the world was round and you and it and you could go on it you could
mf
On - ce the world was roun - d
the world was roun - d
go you could go and you could go on it and you could go on it you could go and you

(half-voice)
mf
you it you it you
and it and you and it you could go and you could go on it and you and it
mf
roun - d roun - d rou -
mf
tim - - e
20
it you it you it it you it it you it you it you it you it you it you it you it
you could go on it and you and it you could go on it and you could go a -
d roun - d roun - d roun - - d roun - d roun - - d
mf
(whistle)
cresc.
it you it you it you it you it you it it you it you it you it you it you
f
dim. poco a poco
round and a - round and a - roun - d a - round and a - round a-round and a - round a -
f (sibilant 'ce')
ce
it you it it you it you it it you it you it
f
mf
f
mf
25
mf dim. poco a poco
round and a - round and a - roun - d a - round and a - round a-round and a - round and a -

77

35
it you it you it you it you it you
worl - - d worl - - d
d rou - nd roun - - d
it it you it you it it you it you
worl - d worl - d
rou - nd rou - nd roun - d
it you it you it you it you it
f f
up - on a time up - on a up - on a time up - on a
rou - nd roun - - d rou - nd
it you it you it it you it you you
f f
up - on a time up - on a up - on a time up - on a
rou - nd roun - - d rou - nd
f dim.
it you it it it you it you it you
it you it it you it you you it you it
f p
up - on a time up - on a worl - - d
ppp p etc.
roun - - - d
On - ce On - ce
mf
ze
40
it it you it you it you it you you
it you it it it
p
Once up - on a time
On - ce On - ce On - ce On - ce On - ce

(whisper)
pp
ti ti ti ti ti ti ti ti ti ti ti ti ti ti ti ti ti ti ti ti ti
the worl - d was round and you and it and you could go on it you could
mf
On - ce On - ce roun - d rou - nd roun -
p
the worl - d was roun - d
45
(half-voice)
ti ti ti ti ti ti ti ti ti ti ti ti the worl - d was round
go you could go you could go you could go you could go you could go
f
d rou - nd rou - nd roun - - d the worl - d was round
tim - e
dim. poco a poco
could and a a and a could a and a could and a a and a could a and a
you could go a-round and a - round and a - roun - d a-round and a - round a -
ppp
etc.
On - ce On - ce On - ce On - ce On - ce
tim - - e
(whistle)
50
a and a could and a a and a could the world was roun - d
round and a-round and a-roun - d a-round and a-roun - d
On - ce ce ce roun - d
ze
(whistle)

Area of Study 2: *Experimental Music*
Treatise: pages 190–191

Cornelius Cardew
(1936–1981)

Extracts from the composer's 'handbook' to *Treatise*:

Treatise is a continuous weaving and combining of a host of graphic elements (of which only a few are recognizably related to musical symbols) into a long visual composition, the meaning of which in terms of sounds is not specified in any way.

I wrote *Treatise* with the definite intention that it should stand entirely on its own, without any form of introduction or instruction to mislead prospective performers into the slavish practice of 'doing what they are told'.

The score must *govern* the music. It must have authority, and not merely be an arbitrary jumping-off point for improvisation, with no internal consistency.

Any number of musicians with any instruments can take part. Each musician plays from the score, reading it in terms of his individual instrument and inclination. A number of general decisions may be made in advance to hold the performance together, but an improvisatory character is essential to the piece. An appreciation or understanding of the piece in performance should grow in much the same way as the musicians' interpretation.

Any rigidity of interpretation is automatically thwarted by the confluence of different personalities.

Cornelius Cardew

The CD has recordings of two different interpretations of pages 190–191.

Cornelius Cardew

Treatise: page 190

Treatise: page 191

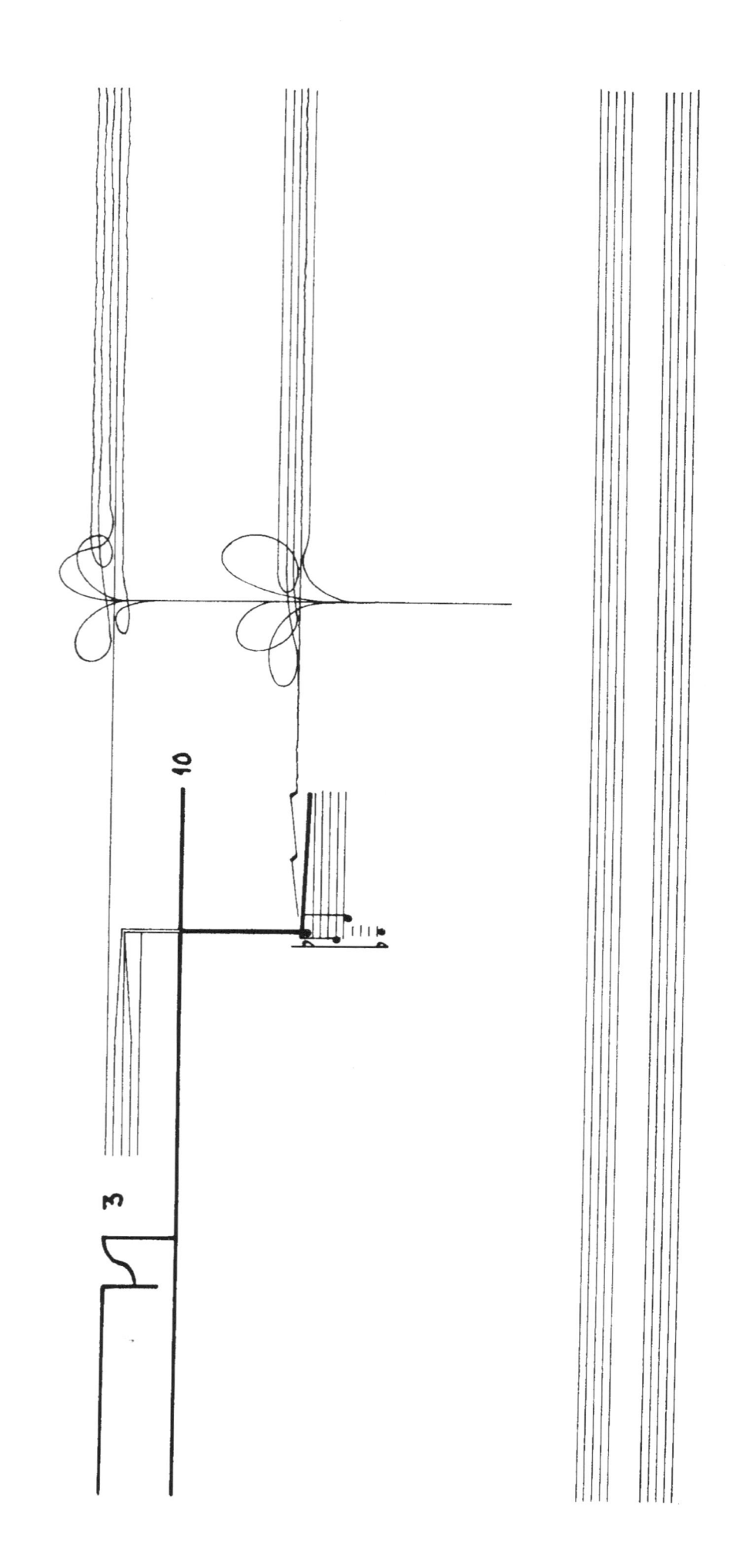

Area of Study 2: *Experimental Music*

'Wa-lie-oh' *from* Songs from the Hill

Meredith Monk (b. 1942)

The following score has been specially prepared to help you follow the recorded performance. It identifies the basic 'cells' of which the piece is composed, and illustrates how these are developed and extended through varied repetition. Empty bars represent the identical repetition of previously heard material, which then 'branches off' in a new variant.

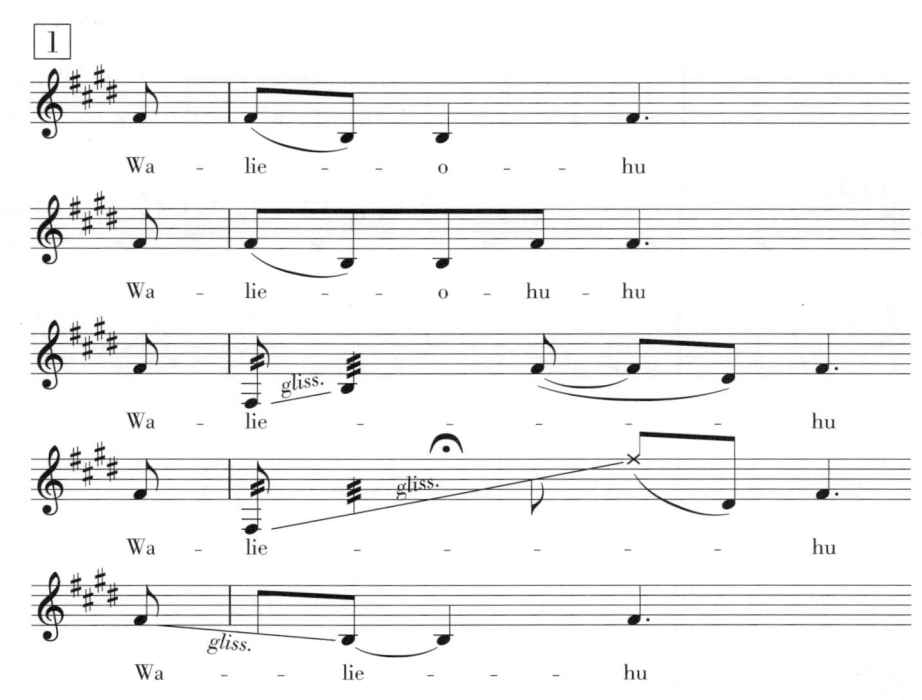

4

Le-lo, le-lo, le-lo, le-lo, le-lo, le-lo, le-lo
Le-lo-lo, le-lo-lo-lo, le - lo, le-lo, le-lo - lo, le - lo, le-lo, le-lo
Le-lo, le-lo, le - lo, le - lo, le - lo, le-lo, le-lo
le-lo, le-lo-lo-lo, le - lo, le-lo, le-lo, le-lo, le - lo, le-lo-lo, le-lo, le - lo, le-lo, le-lo

5

Le-lo, le-lo, le-lo, um-le
um-le le
um-le-le, um - le
um-le-le, um-le - le, um - le
um-le-lo, um - le-le - le, um - le-le - le, um - le
le-le - le, le-le-le um-le
um-le-le, um-ba, um-ba
um-le-le, um-ba, um-ba, um-ba, um-ba, um-le - le, um-ba, um-ba, um-le-le, um-le-le, um-ba, um-ba
um-le-le, um-le - le, um-le - le, um-le - le um-le - le, um-le-le um-le-le, um-le - le

The composer has written:

'I never made scores for any of the *Songs from the Hill*. They are solo pieces and part of the joy of singing them is the combination of rigour and freedom. The forms are set but within them there is always room to explore.

'I think of the piece as a tree with three different branches, or as a modified rondo form. After each variation there is a return to the "lay-lo" [le-lo] figure, although even within that there are specific rhythmic variations each time it is sung.'

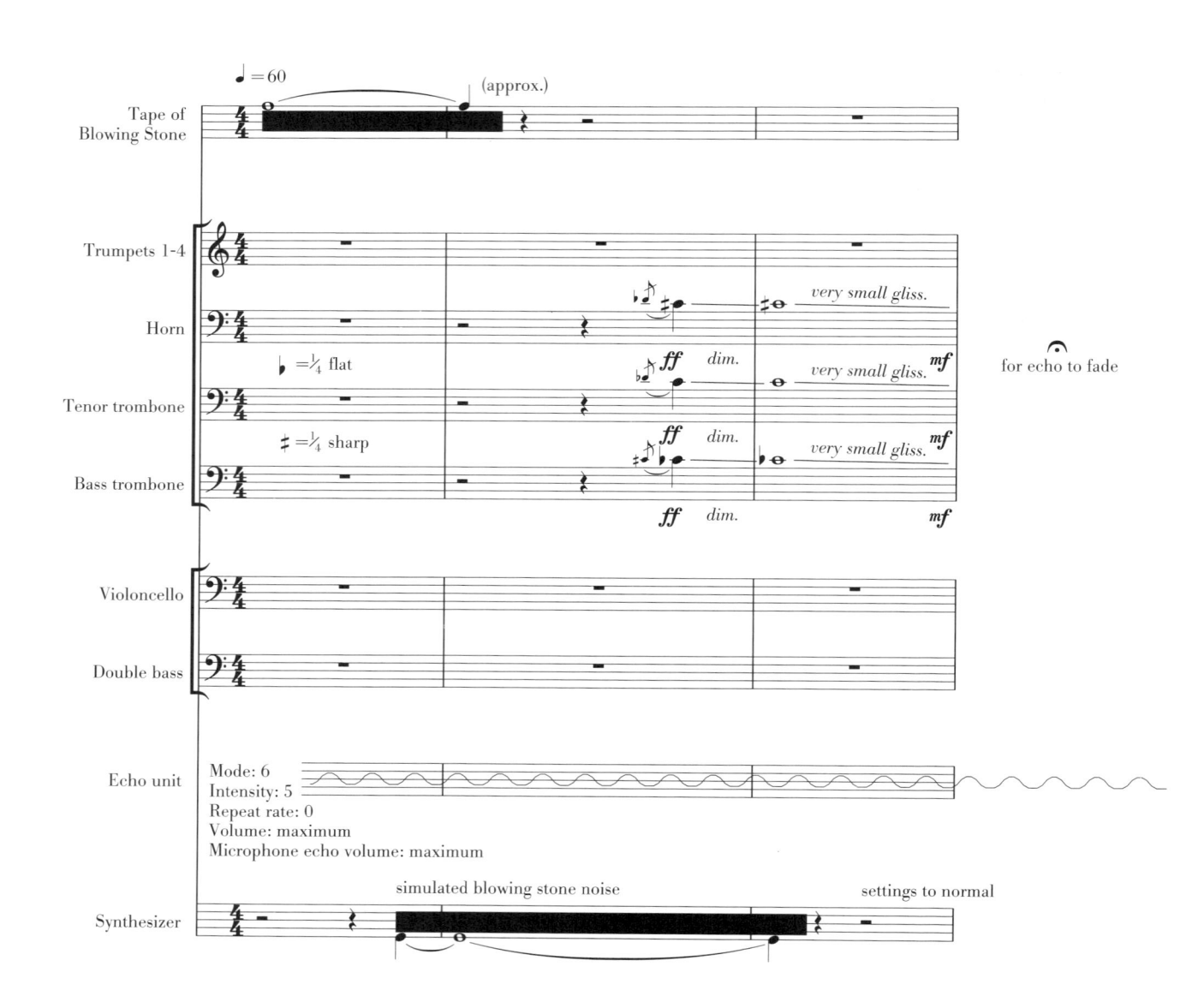

Area of Study 2: *Electronic Music*

The Song of the White Horse: 'The Blowing Stone'

David Bedford
(b. 1937)

The Song of the White Horse is a musical evocation of the Ridgeway footpath between Wayland's Smithy (a Stone Age burial chamber) and the White Horse of Uffington, a hillside carving. The Blowing Stone is a large stone that creates a siren-like sound when the wind blows through it. The composition culminates in a setting of words from the *The Ballad of the White Horse* by G. K. Chesterton, celebrating King Alfred's victory over the Danes in the 9th century. *The Blowing Stone* is the third of five sections.

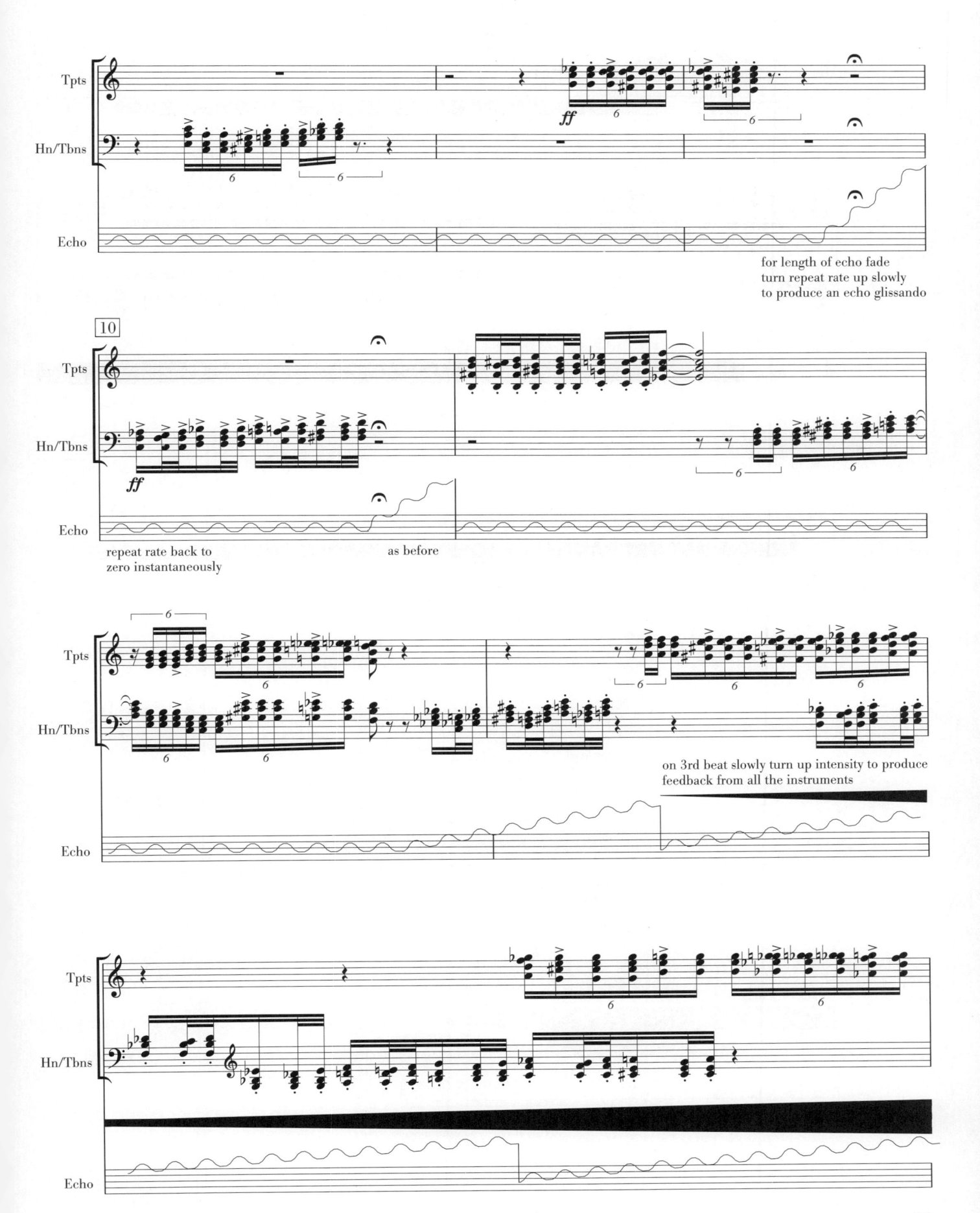

for length of echo fade
turn repeat rate up slowly
to produce an echo glissando

10

repeat rate back to
zero instantaneously

as before

on 3rd beat slowly turn up intensity to produce
feedback from all the instruments

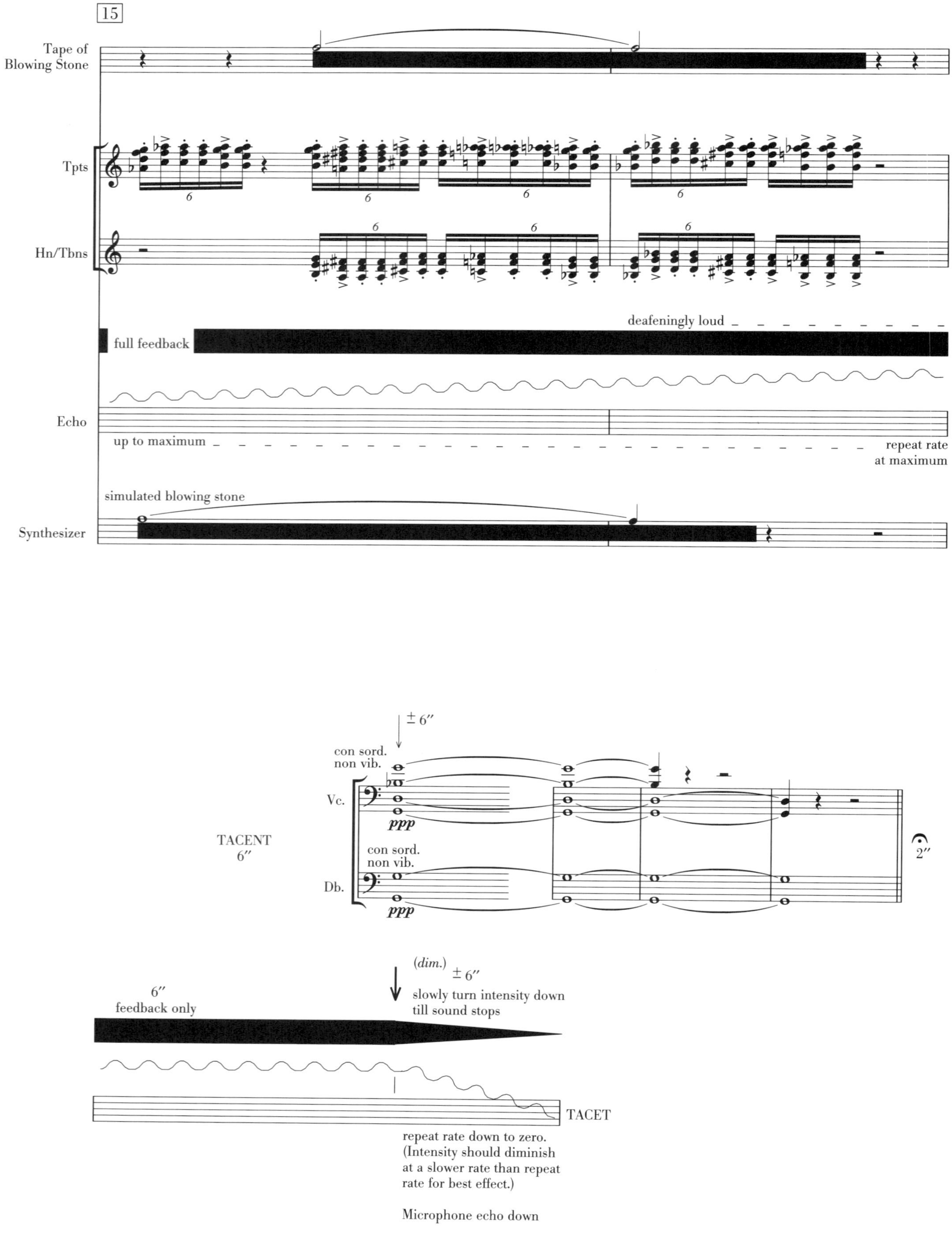
15
Tape of Blowing Stone
Tpts
6
Hn/Tbns
full feedback
deafeningly loud
Echo
up to maximum
repeat rate at maximum
simulated blowing stone
Synthesizer
± 6″
con sord. non vib.
Vc.
ppp
TACENT 6″
con sord. non vib.
Db.
ppp
2″
(dim.)
6″ feedback only
slowly turn intensity down till sound stops
TACET
repeat rate down to zero. (Intensity should diminish at a slower rate than repeat rate for best effect.)
Microphone echo down

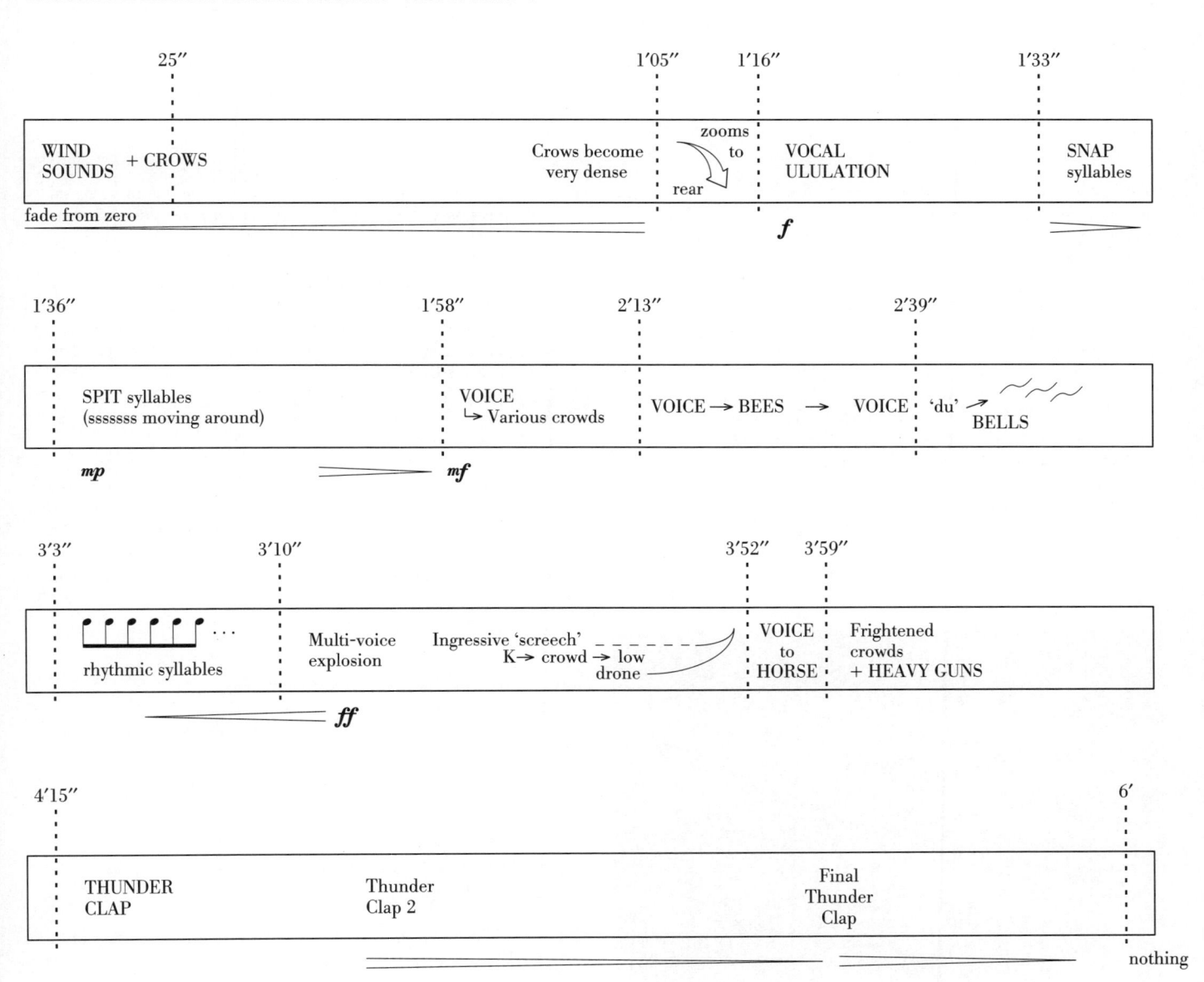

Area of Study 2: *Electronic Music*
Vox 5

Trevor Wishart
(b. 1946)

Vox 5 is the fifth in a cycle of six vocal pieces dealing with many different aspects of what it is to be 'human', and using the voice as the focus of this exploration. The piece takes vocal sounds and, through computer technology, creates what the composer calls a 'supervoice', which metamorphoses into other sounds: bells, crows, crowds, bees and less recognizable events.

The cycle of pieces is influenced by the image of the Hindu god Shiva, a many-limbed figure dancing in a circle of fire, and the composer writes of this music as 'images of the creation and destruction of the world contained within the "voice of Shiva"'.

The piece was originally submitted as a project to IRCAM, the computer music centre in Paris, in 1979–84, but it could not be realized until 1986 because of the changing nature of the technology at the time. Sound data is stretched and manipulated by computer programs written by the composer, and which he describes as new musical instruments.

In the four-channel version the sound travels from front centre stage all around the auditorium, apparently ejected from the mouth of Shiva.

Time	Event
25″	WIND SOUNDS + CROWS (fade from zero)
1′05″	Crows become very dense
1′16″	zooms to rear — VOCAL ULULATION (*f*)
1′33″	SNAP syllables
1′36″	SPIT syllables (sssssss moving around) (*mp*)
1′58″	VOICE → Various crowds (*mf*)
2′13″	VOICE → BEES
2′39″	VOICE 'du' → BELLS
3′3″	rhythmic syllables
3′10″	Multi-voice explosion — Ingressive 'screech' K→ crowd → low drone (*ff*)
3′52″	VOICE to HORSE
3′59″	Frightened crowds + HEAVY GUNS
4′15″	THUNDER CLAP
	Thunder Clap 2
	Final Thunder Clap
6′	nothing

89

Area of Study 2: *Electronic Music*
Hyde Park

Toby Bricheno
(b. 1965)

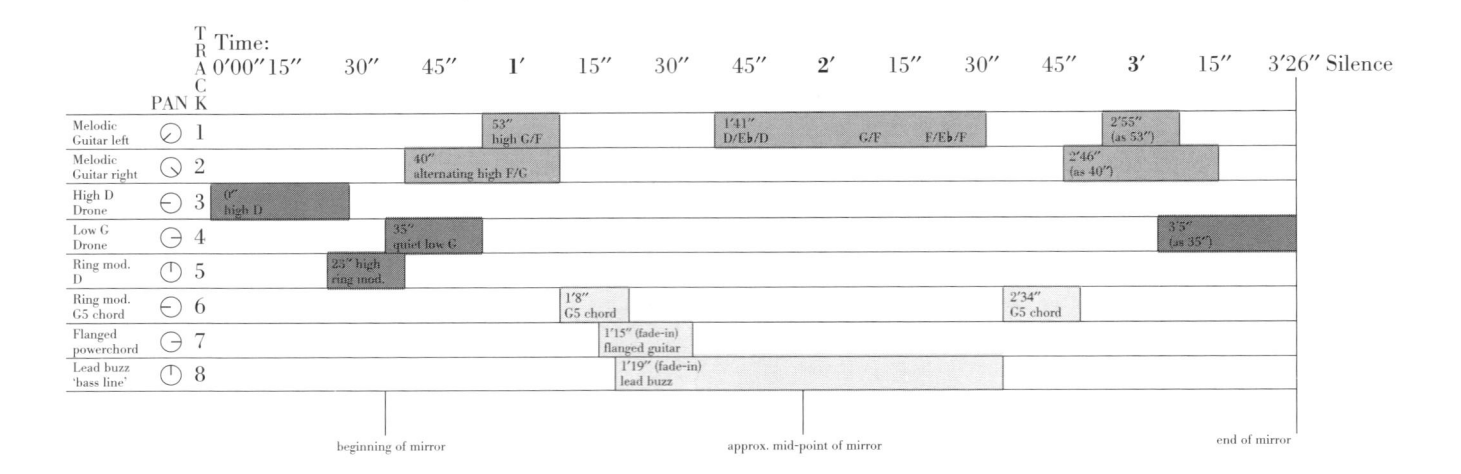

Track	PAN	0'00"	15"	30"	45"	1'	15"	30"	45"	2'	15"	30"	45"	3'	15"	3'26" Silence
Melodic Guitar left	1 (L)					53" high G/F				1'41" D/E♭/D		G/F	F/E♭/F	2'55" (as 53")		
Melodic Guitar right	2 (R)			40" alternating high F/G										2'46" (as 40")		
High D Drone	3 (C)	0" high D														
Low G Drone	4 (C)				35" quiet low G									3'5" (as 35")		
Ring mod. D	5 (C)		25" high ring mod.													
Ring mod. G5 chord	6 (L)						1'8" G5 chord					2'34" G5 chord				
Flanged powerchord	7 (R)						1'15" (fade-in) flanged guitar									
Lead buzz 'bass line'	8 (C)							1'19" (fade-in) lead buzz								

beginning of mirror — approx. mid-point of mirror — end of mirror

This piece was originally composed to be used as part of a multimedia installation with photographer Sheila Brannigan. The accompanying photographs are of different views of the dark and sinister-looking subway complex at Hyde Park Corner.

It was written and recorded using electric guitars, a Boss GT-3 guitar effects processor and an Apple Macintosh G4 computer running Emagic Logic Audio Platinum Software. To achieve some of the sounds, three effects in particular were employed:

1. An Ebow is used extensively on tracks 1–5. This is a device which is held on the guitar string and drives it with an electromagnetic field causing it to sustain for as long as the Ebow is held in place.
2. A ring modulator was used on tracks 5 and 6. Ring modulation is a process whereby the audio signal is modulated by an oscillator, resulting in a unique bell-like sound.
3. A Pitch Shifter, which enables the pitch of the incoming signal to be transposed. This was used on track 6 to lower the G5 chord by an octave.

While using the Pitch Shifter I noticed that if I touched the end of my guitar lead, a low frequency note was produced. Every time I touched the lead the frequency changed. It reminded me of a slow-moving passacaglia bass line and this is the sound that 'performed' the bass on track 8.

Panning, stereo reverb and delay were used on each track to add a sense of space and eeriness.

The piece was freely improvised and has strong references to a G minor tonality. Initially I recorded about 10 minutes of solo guitar improvisation, using the Ebow, ring modulator and Pitch Shifter from the Boss GT-3. I then listened back, picking out sections that I liked and combining them into the eight tracks you see on the score.

Journey: Hyde Park Subway

Structure

0'0"   high and low drones on the note D

40"   more melodic elements emerge forming a simple duet

1'8"   G5 chord signals start of next section

1'19"   bass line fades in

1'41"   Ebow melody over the bass line suggesting a G minor tonality

2'34"   G5 chord announces start of mirror section – music from 40" to 1'8" is recapitulated in reverse order

3'26"   silence

AREA OF STUDY 3

Popular Song in Context

12-Bar Blues
Reggae
Club Dance Remix
Songs from Musicals

Area of Study 3: *12-Bar Blues*

WPA Blues

W. Weldon, L. Melrose

as recorded by Casey Bill Weldon, 1936

WPA Blues was recorded on 12 February 1936, by Casey Bill Weldon (vocal, guitar), Black Bob (piano), and a bass player unknown.

'WPA' stands for Works Progress Administration. This was a nationally funded agency, one of many elements forming President Franklin D. Roosevelt's 'New Deal'. Its main aim was to provide jobs for the unemployed, to counteract the effects of the economic depression which had hit America hard since the Wall Street Crash of 1929.

By the end of 1935 the WPA was providing jobs for some 3 million people, albeit on low wages. However, there were sometimes people who lost as well as those who gained: *WPA Blues* describes the situation of a man who rents a room in a house designated for slum-clearance by a WPA works team. The song describes the double-bind whereby the welfare agency will pay his existing rent, but slum-clearance condemns his home to demolition; yet being unemployed further prevents him from finding a new home. A number of other blues songs were written about the WPA, some thankful for the work it provided, but others critical of various aspects of the programme and how it operated in practice.

The chords used in the introduction and the first two verses are set out above the words, on the next page. Verse 1 follows a typical form of the classic 12-bar structure, harmonically and in its poetic structure.

In verses 2–5 a common variant is followed. In effect, the chord pattern of line 1 of each verse is extended from 4 bars to 8, all on chord I (A major in this case):

I	I	I	I	I	I	I	I
IV	IV	I	I				
V	V	I	I				

The extended first line carries most of the narrative, and is sung almost entirely on just two notes. The final two lines then have the character of a refrain, and are sung more lyrically.

Casey Bill used the then-popular 'Hawaiian' style of steel-guitar playing, laying the guitar flat on his lap and using a bottle-neck to 'stop' the strings with the left hand. The introduction could be notated as follows, with C sharps mostly slurred from C natural:

For the rest of the song he plays short phrases between the vocal lines, just enough to underpin the harmony and rhythm.

The bass plays mostly on the first and third beats, for instance:

The piano plays rather in the background, and fulfils a harmonic role, for instance turning the bassist's D into a D⁷ harmony with this figure (verse 2 bar 9):

Intro.

chords:

| A | E | A E | A |

Verse 1

| A | A | A | A⁷ |
Everybody's workin' in this town, and it's worried me night and day,

| D⁷ | D⁷ | A | A |
Everybody's workin' in this town, and it's worried me night and day,

| E | E | A | A |
It's that mean workin' crew, that works for the WPA.

Verse 2

| A | A | A | A |
Well, well, the landlord come this morning, and he knocked on my door, He asked me if I was goin' to pay my rent no more.

| A | A | A | A⁷ |
He said, 'You have to move, if you can't pay.' And then he turned, and he walked slowly away.

| D⁷ | D⁷ | A | A |
So I have to try, find me some other place to stay,

| E | E | A | A |
That house wreckin' crew is coming, from that WPA.

3   Well, well, I went to the relief station, and I didn't have a cent,
       They said, 'Stay on where you're stayin', you don't have to pay no rent.'
       So when I got back home, they was tackin' a notice on the door:
       'This house is condemned, and you can't live here no more.'
So a notion struck me, I'd better be on my way,
They're gonna tear my house down, oo-ooh, that crew from that WPA.

4   Well, well, I went out next morning, I put a lock on my door,
       But though I wouldn't move, but I had no place to go,
       The real estate people, they all done got so,
       They don't rent to, no relief clients no more,
So I know, have to walk the streets night and day,
Because that wreckin' crew's coming, oo-ooh, from that WPA

5   Well, well, a notion struck me, I'd try to stay a day or two,
       But I soon found out, that that wouldn't do,
       Early next morning, while I was layin' in my bed,
       I heard a mighty rumblin', and bricks come tumblin' down on my head,
So I had to start duckin' and dodgin', and be on my way,
They was tearin' my house down on me, oo-ooh, that crew from that WPA.

Area of Study 3: *12-Bar Blues*

I know you lied
as recorded by Bill Thomas, 2001

Bill Thomas

When songs are transcribed from their original recordings, they are often reduced to a vocal melody line with chord symbols, as here. To some extent the notation is approximate – the pitches and rhythms aren't exact – but a 'lead sheet' of this sort is an important record of the song for copyright purposes, or as a reminder of how the song goes.

Db7 May come as a shock,
Db7 As chan-ges oft - en do
Db7 I've had e-nough ba - by,
65
Db7 I've had e-nough of your lies too,
Gb7 ly - in' to me,
Gb7 Mmm Ev' - ry
Db7 now and then.
Db7
Ab7 I get the feel - in' ba - by
70
Gb7 ly - in's your
Db7 best friend.
Db7
Guitar solo 12
85
Guitar solo 12
Coda
Ab7 Search the skies for sun-ny days,
Gb7 The rain keeps
Db7 com - in' down.
100
Db7
Ab7 One day you'll look for true love
Gb7 But a ly - in' love is
Db7 all you'll find.
105
Db7 Ab7 Gb7 Db
Bass Guitar
x 8
Coda

Area of Study 3: *Reggae*
Freedom Fighters
as recorded by Delroy Washington, 1976

Delroy Washington

The structure of the song is very simple. An introduction is followed by alternating choruses and verses, punctuated by a guitar solo after the third chorus. The four-bar chord progression remains the same throughout the song.

Oh yeah, oh yeah, oh yeah, oh yeah,
Well, well, oh yeah

CHORUS

Get up, you a freedom fighters
Aye, it's time you got up on your feet
Get up, you a freedom fighters
Aye, it's time you got up on your feet

You're fighting your brother every day-ay
And I'm sure that ain't the way, yeah
You're robbing your mother daily
And I'm sure that ain't a way to treat a lady

CHORUS

You tell me you love your sister
And then why send her out on the streets
You're saying you'd like to make ends meet
But you're bound to knock her off her feet

CHORUS

GUITAR SOLO

CHORUS

The bass drum sounds on the second and fourth beats of the bar, as is usual in reggae. These beats are further accented by rim shots on the snare drum. Occasional offbeats are picked out by the drummer, again using rim shots.

The guitar plays one of the hallmarks of reggae – repeated offbeat quaver notes. *Barre* (or bar) chords are used which enable the guitarist to mute the strings with the left hand, resulting in a choppier, more percussive sound. The bass, possibly the most important instrument in reggae, plays the same four-bar pattern throughout, with a few minor variations in the penultimate bar of the pattern. The rhythm is mostly in quavers and semiquavers.

The clavinet, a keyboard instrument, plays a three-note 'hook' in most bars; the rest of the time it shadows the bass. The organ, on the other hand, is used almost as a percussion instrument – it plays a typical reggae keyboard part with one hand on top of the other in order to re-trigger the same notes with greater speed.

There is much repetition in the vocal line. Note the use of the minor 3rd (D) and flattened 7th (A) throughout. This type of simple melodic line is heard often in reggae (e.g. 'Get up, stand up' by Bob Marley). Also, notice the 'blue' note (the F♮) which is derived from North American blues.

Area of Study 3: *Reggae*

Real Rock

C. S. Dodd

as recorded by Sound Dimension

This track has many features that are typical of reggae music. It is in 4/4 and is scored for guitar, bass guitar, piano, organ, trombone and drums. It has a characteristic rhythmic texture where the drums accent the second and fourth crotchets of each bar. The bass plays a one-bar pattern based on only two pitches, mainly made up of semiquavers (16th-notes). The percussive offbeat quavers in the guitar part are reinforced by the piano, which occasionally also varies the rhythm slightly. The organ plays a three-note motif. Much of the material is repeated and the harmony is limited to two chords.

98

Area of Study 3: *Club Dance Remix*

Spellbound

M. Rae, S. Christian, B. Green, D. Pomeranz

as recorded by Rae & Christian, featuring Veba (Mix 1) Rae & Christian remix, 1998

The CD includes three different mixes of Spellbound. The original song has been reinterpreted through the use of technology. 'Remixes' originated in the early 1980s as part of the dance movement. Record producers would take an original track and remix it, changing the balance and style, sometimes adding new ingredients, and sometimes taking away elements of the original.

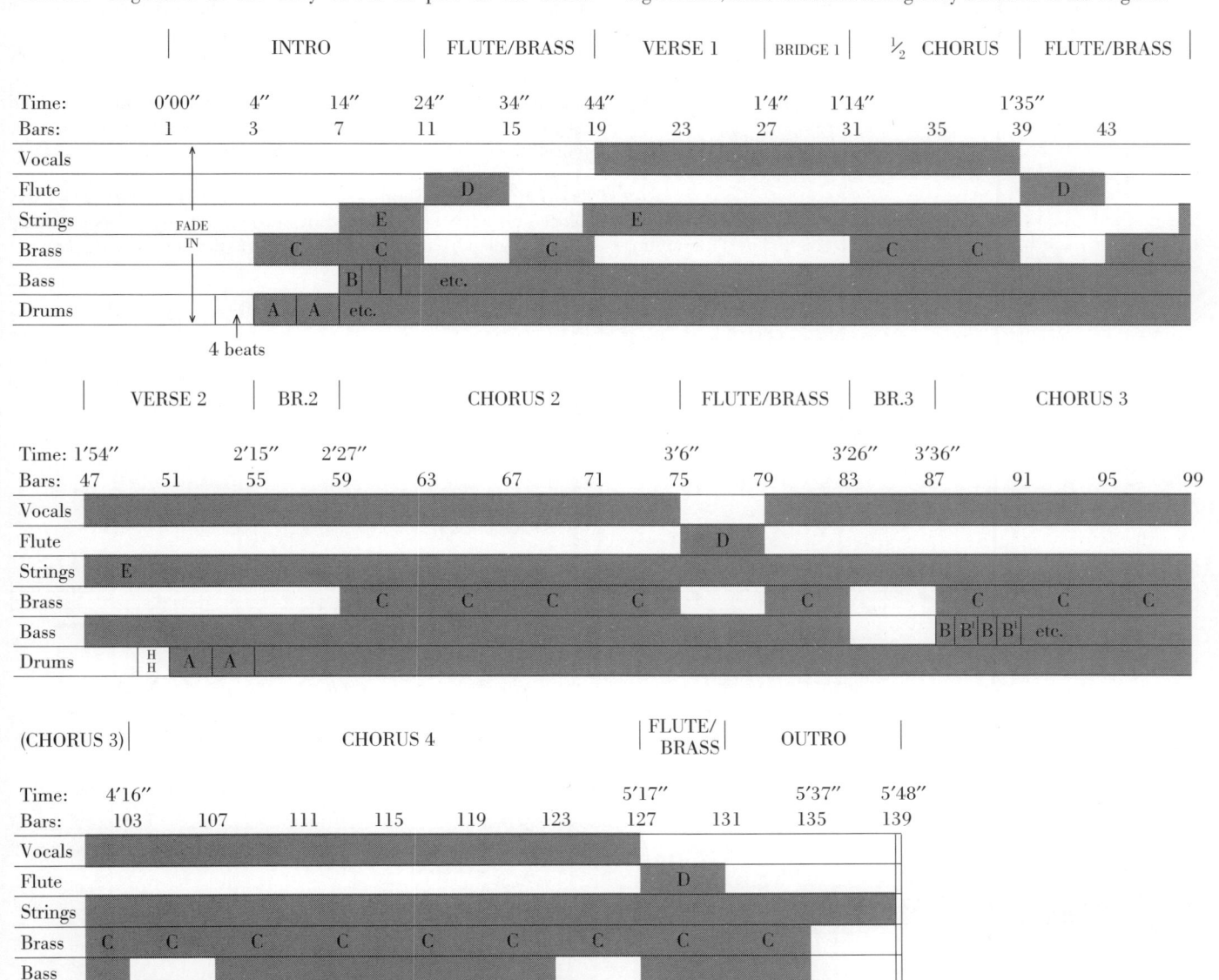

[Structural diagram showing sections: INTRO, FLUTE/BRASS, VERSE 1, BRIDGE 1, ½ CHORUS, FLUTE/BRASS, VERSE 2, BR.2, CHORUS 2, FLUTE/BRASS, BR.3, CHORUS 3, CHORUS 4, FLUTE/BRASS, OUTRO with timings and bar numbers, and instrumental parts for Vocals, Flute, Strings, Brass, Bass, Drums]

Verse 1
It's too much to comprehend, beyond what you'd imagine
I'm enchanted by your magic caught in a spell that never ends

Chorus (half)
I cannot run, I will not hide
I'm holding my head high
It's your good love releases me
Submit, I cannot fight
You got me, you got me
So hooked upon your love
You got me, you got me
I'm yours completely, I'm spellbound
Your love, your love, it's got me.

Verse 2
I'm trying to define what you do to me
I'm rising to the sky like a bird flying free

Chorus (full)
I cannot run, I will not hide
I'm holding my hands high
It's your good love releases me
Submit, I cannot fight
You got me, you got me
So hooked upon your love
You got me, you got me
I'm yours completely, I'm spellbound
Your love, your love, it's got me
You got me, you got me
So hooked upon your love
You got me, you got me
I'm yours completely, I'm spellbound
Your love, your love, it's got me.

This mix largely follows a standard pop song format, comprising verses, bridges and choruses punctuated by instrumental passages (flute break [D]). The bass [B] and drums [A] consist of a one-bar and two-bar loop respectively, and form a rhythmic foundation for the whole song.

Note how the bass and drums (and to a lesser extent the brass [C]) are closely related rhythmically. All the parts make use of syncopation with the exception of the string part [E], which forms a serene contrast to the rest of the track.

The bass and drums often drop out of the arrangement, e.g. drums at bar 47 (1′54″) and bass at bar 83 (3′27″). This imitates the muting and unmuting of a channel on a mixing desk (originally found in reggae dub mixes), and draws attention to the bass frequencies or 'bottom end' when either the bass or drums re-enter. This will be particularly noticeable on a club PA system, which is capable of producing powerful bass frequencies.

You may notice that most of the parts consist of looped passages between one and four bars in length. This is common in many forms of dance music, and is partly a result of the way in which digital samples and sequences can be easily looped on computer sequencing software. In fact, writing music on computers positively encourages this approach. It is also because memory was comparatively limited on the first samplers and the samples could only be a bar or two in length. This has had a lasting effect on dance music, and the use of short loops is still very popular.

The four-crotchet figure at bar 2 is another example of the way dance music has been affected by music technology. This pounding effect is called 're-triggering' and refers to the constant triggering of a sample, generally by MIDI.

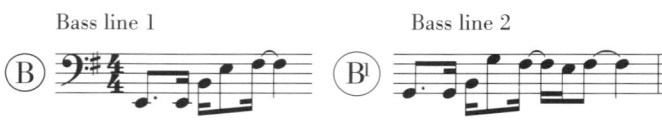

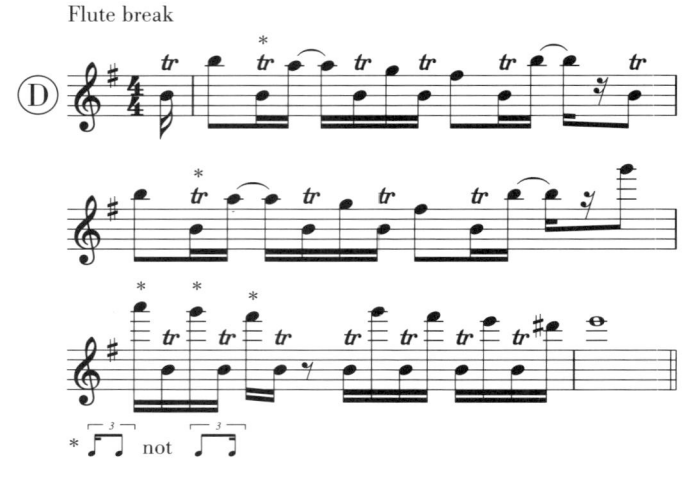

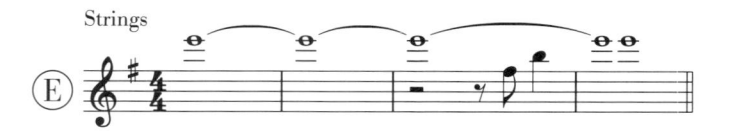

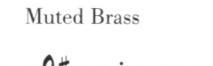

Area of Study 3: *Club Dance Remix*

Spellbound

M. Rae, S. Christian, B. Green, D. Pomeranz

(Mix 2) Rae & Christian remix dub, 1998

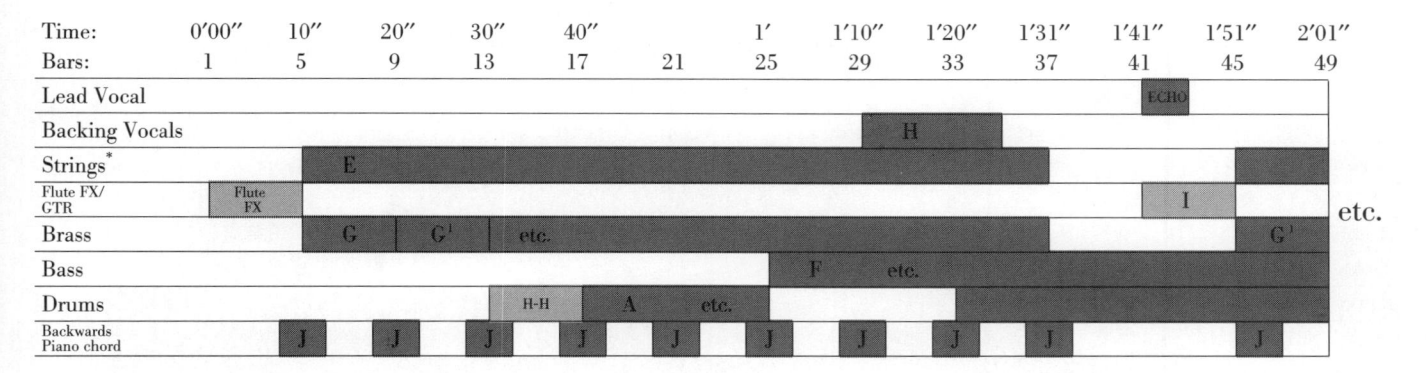

Time:	0'00"	10"	20"	30"	40"	1'	1'10"	1'20"	1'31"	1'41"	1'51"	2'01"
Bars:	1	5	9	13	17	21	25	29	33	37	41	45	49

The structure of Mix 2 is looser than that of Mix 1, with less clearly defined sections. There is no real sense of verse/bridge/chorus. It is more of a collage in which a series of episodes is assembled over a near-constant foundation of drums and bass.

Vocals are markedly less prominent, with only a fragment of the verse vocal used. This is altered dramatically by the use of a digital delay on the voice at bar 41.

Conversely, much use is made of the chorus backing vocals (or B.V.s) [H]. It is not unusual to use only the vocal 'hooks' in a remix, and sometimes these are the only recognizable elements from the original mix.

The bass [F] and drums are even more prominent than in the first mix and at bars 37–40 they are the only instruments playing. An entirely new bass line has been substituted for the original – in fact, many of the parts from the first mix are absent altogether.

Many of the new sounds are quite distinctive, e.g. the piano which is played-back backwards [J] and the echo brass [G]. Note that the brass builds up a more complex rhythm as it progresses. This is very similar to a technique employed by the minimalist composers such as Steve Reich. In this case the increase in complexity is achieved by electronic means. The rhythmically simple brass part is sent to a digital delay. The resultant combination of 'dry' and delayed signals is much more interesting than the initial brass part. The effect is further intensified by panning the delayed signal between left and right speakers.

Notice how the guitar part [I] often plays on beats where the bass is resting. Combined with the bass it adds to the feeling of rhythmic syncopation (or 'funkiness'), a key goal of dance music generally.

101

Area of Study 3: *Club Dance Remix*

Spellbound

(Mix 3) Old English remix by Andy Madhatter and Si Brad, 1998

M. Rae, S. Christian, B. Green, D. Pomeranz

CD3 Track: 7

| | INTRO | TINKLE PIANO BREAK/ B.V. | VERSE 1 | BRIDGE 1 | CHORUS 1 | TINKLE PIANO BREAK/ B.V. | |

Time: 0'00" 10" 20" 40" 1' 1'10" 1'31" 1'51" 2'01"
Bars: 1 5 9 13 17 21 25 29 33 37 41 45 49

(Chart showing parts: Lead Vocal, Backing Vocals, Tinkle Piano, Funky Piano, Phazed Strings, Thin Bass, Deep Bass, Guitar, Drums — with labels H, P, L, M, O, O², O¹, N, K, H-H claps, B.V. double, etc.)

In terms of structure this is much closer to Mix 1 than Mix 2 and is again based on a standard pop song format. The original vocals remain more or less intact (however, note the vocal-less outro from bar 93 (3'52") to the end) and the drums and bass hardly drop out at all. The tinkle piano break (bar 9, 37 and 73) performs a similar role to the flute/brass break in the original mix.

The thin bass [L], funk guitar [N] and piano [P] interlock rhythmically, in much the same way as the bass and guitar parts in Mix 2. However, in terms of sonority this mix is different from both Mixes 1 and 2.

The drums [K] are simpler but have a handclap on beats 2 and 4, giving them a stronger hip-hop feel. Also, chord progressions have been introduced – Bm7 and Em in the verse, Em7 and C#m7 in the bridge. There are also new bass lines ([L] and [M]) which follow the chord progression in the bridge section.

The deep bass [O] which enters at bar 9 (20") adds dramatically to the bass frequencies and will be particularly noticeable on a club PA system.

Note the increase in rhythmic impetus at bridge 1 (bar 25, 1') when the deep bass doubles in speed.

Drums

(K) ♩ = snare drum + handclap

Deep Bass

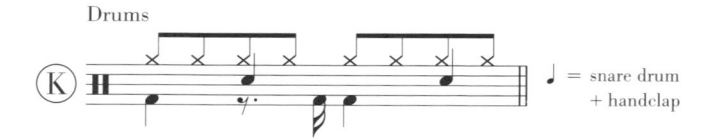

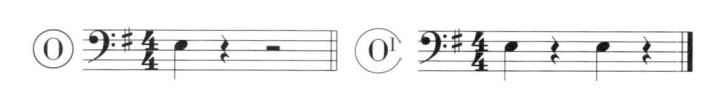

(O)

Deep Bass 2

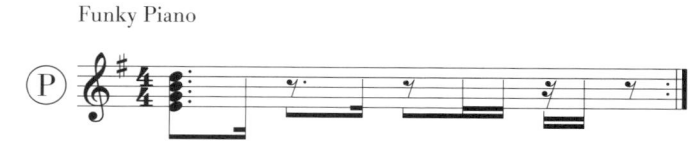

(O¹)

Thin Bass

(L)

Deep Bass bridge

(O²) |1. |2.

Bass bridge

(M)

Funky Piano

(P)

Funk Guitar

(N)

102

Area of Study 3: *Club Dance Remix*
Cosmic Interlude

D. Williamson

as recorded by LTJ Bukem, 1997

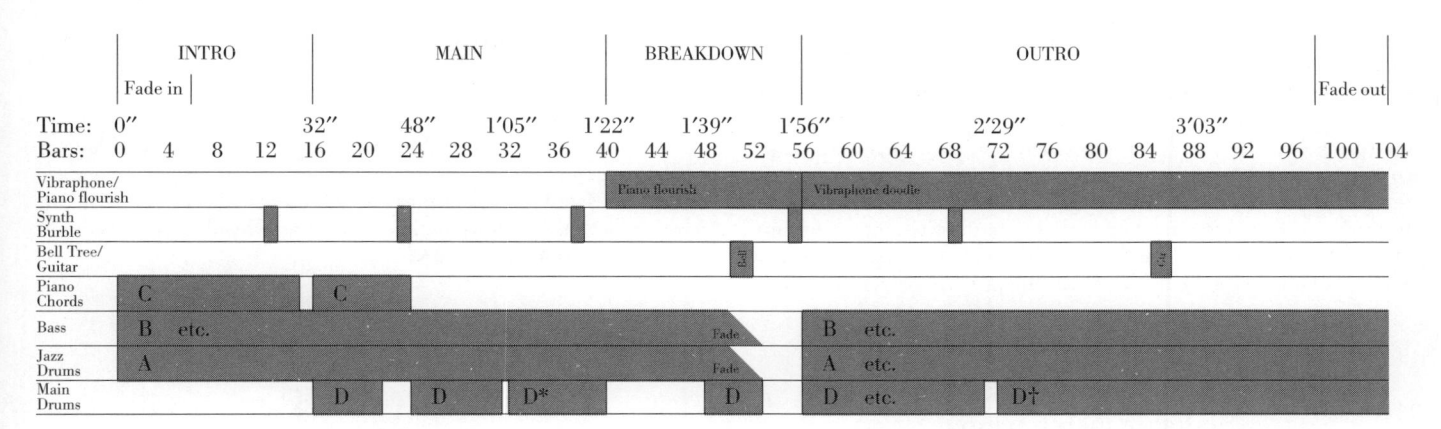

Main Drums from bar 31

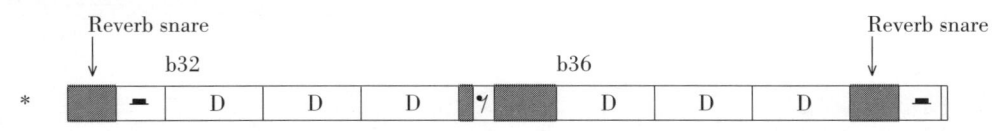

Main Drums from bar 70

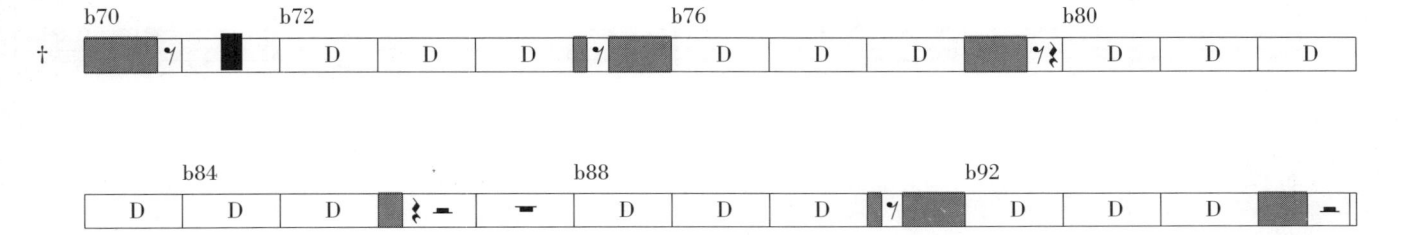

This has a similar collage structure to *Spellbound* Mix 2, in that there is no real sense of verse/bridge/chorus. Again it is more of a series of episodes over a foundation of continuous drums and bass.

As before, much use is made of muting and unmuting the main drums (see inset examples of bars 31–39 and 70–95). The occasional use of heavy reverb on the snare drum is another technique originating from reggae dub mixing and used extensively in dance music production. This mix makes use of two contrasting drum loops: an initially light and jazzy loop [A] is complemented by a heavier and bassier hip-hop type loop [D].

The gentle intro section is followed by the main section. The rhythm section drops out during the soft breakdown section, but is reintroduced for the outro.

Note how the bass [B] and drums ([A] and [D]) are the most continuous elements of the mix.

Again there is extensive use of interesting and unusual sounds – the synthesizer burble, bell tree and guitar, which all help to punctuate the mix. The vibraphone sound (bar 56, 1′56′′) and extended harmonies of the piano chords [C] lend the piece a jazzy dimension.

Area of Study 3: *Songs from Musicals*
'Consider Yourself' *from* 'Oliver!'

Lionel Bart
(1930–1999)

You will hear that the performance on the CD differs in many details from the simple piano score given. Orchestral embellishments are prominent: for example, the flutes on the words 'It's clear we're (going to get along)'. The piano score forms the basis of the recorded interpretation. It has been included so that you can make comparisons and create your own version.

In the recording there are four verses. The first two are sung in G major; the third is in C major, and the final verse is in B♭ major. Verse 1 is sung as a solo, by the Artful Dodger, whereas in Verse 2 the lyrics are shared between two voices: the Artful Dodger and Oliver. Verses 3 and 4 are sung by a chorus comprising the Londoners and street urchins.

Verse 3 features the most striking departures from the score. Some of the lyrics are omitted, for example the second line 'Consider yourself one of the family'. Furthermore, at the points where the lyrics are missing, new music in triple time is introduced with lots of shouting and whistling from the singers.

20
F F♯° Gm7 C7 F F+7 B♭
clear we're go - ing to get a - long! Con - sid - er Your - self
F7 B♭ 25 B°
well in: Con - sid - er Your - self part of the
Cm7 F7 F+7 B♭ 30 D7 Gm
fur - ni - ture. There is - n't a lot to spare;
35
G♯° F F♯° Gm7 C7 F F7
Who cares? What - ev - er we've got we share! If it should
No - bod - y

chance to be we should see some harder days, Empty larder days, why grouse?
tries to be lah-di-dah and uppity, There's a cup o' tea for all. Always a chance we'll meet somebody to foot the bill, Then the drinks are on the house!
Only it's wise to be handy wiv a rolling pin, When the landlord comes to call!

Consider Yourself our mate, We

Cm G+7 Cm 60 A7 B♭ A Gm7 A6
don't want to have no fuss For aft - er some con -
B♭ A6 Gm7 A B♭ Fm6 G7 1. 65 Cm7 F7
- sid - er - a - tion, we can state: Con - sid - er Your - self one of
B♭ B° F7 F+7 2. Cm 70
us. Con - sid - er Your - self
mf
cresc.
F7 B♭ 75
one of us.
ff

Area of Study 3 — *Songs from Musicals*
'Cabaret' *from* Cabaret

John Kander (b. 1927) and
Fred Ebb (b. 1932)

cue: . . . Fraülein Sally Bowles!

20
-ret, old chum, Come to the cab - a - ret.
Brass
Acc.
Brass
+ Cls
25
Put down the knit - ting, the book and the broom.
Acc.
p
Cls
Brass muted
30
Time for a hol - i - day.
Life is a
(Acc. cont. melody)
Brass
Cls div.
35
cab - a - ret, old chum, Come to the cab - a -
Brass
Acc.

40
-ret. Come taste the wine, Come hear the
Acc., Cls
Brass, W.w.
Gtr
45
Slower
Poco rall.
band. Come blow a horn, start cel-e-brat-ing; Right this way, your
Cls
A tempo
50
ta-ble's wait-ing. No use per-mit-ting some pro-phet of doom To
Acc.
Cls
Brass
55
wipe ev-'ry smile a-way. Life is a
Brass
+ Cls
Cls

60
cab - a - ret, old chum, Come to the cab - a -
Brass
Slightly faster
65
- ret!
I used to have a
f
Tbn
Acc.
Cls
p
70
girl - friend known as El - sie,
With whom I shared four sor - did rooms in
Cls
+ W.Blk
Tbns
f
Cls
p
75
Chel - sea.
She was - n't what you'd call a blush - ing flow - er.
Cls
+Tbns
f
Cls
Tbns
3

As a matter of fact she rented by the hour. The day she died the neighbors came to snicker: 'Well, that's what comes of too much pills and liquor.' But when I saw her laid out like a queen, She was the happiest corpse I'd ever seen. I think of El-sie to this ve-ry day. I re-mem-ber how she'd turn to me and say:

Slowly – In 2

'What good is sit-ting a-lone in your room? Come hear the mu-sic play. Life is a cab-a-ret, old chum, Come to the cab-a-ret.

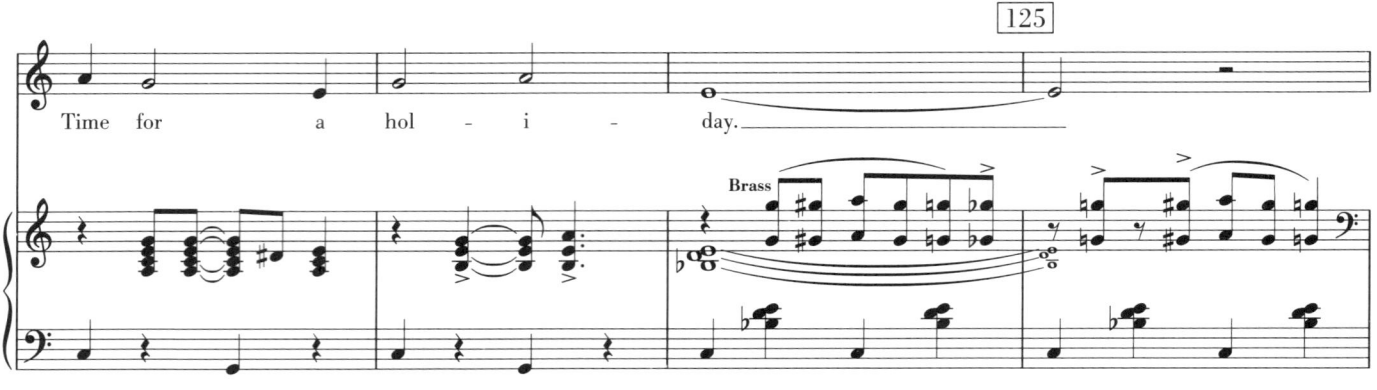

Put down the knit-ting, the book and the broom,____ Time for a hol-i-day.____

Life is a cab-a-ret, old chum,____ Come to the cab-a-ret.' And as for me,

135
ad lib. (deliberately)
as for me, I made my mind up, back in Chelsea,
Str., Acc.
gliss.
140
Cake-walk (Slower)
+ Str.
When I go I'm go-ing like El-sie. Start by ad-mit-ting, from
Tpt Solo (Harmon mute)
+Saxs
Saxs
145
Accel.
cra-dle to tomb
Is-n't that long a
etc.
(Tempo I)
150
Accel. poco a poco
Tpt Solo
stay.
Life is a cab-a-
+Saxs, Hn, Tbns
Acc.
Saxs

155
-ret, old chum, On - ly a cab - a -
Tbn
160
-ret, old chum, And I love a cab - -
Brass octaves
Tbn
- a - - ret.
Vlns
ff Brass, Saxs, Acc.
+Tom-toms
165
Banjo gliss.
+Tbns, Bar.

AREA OF STUDY 4

Rhythms, Scales and Modes in Music from Around the World

Gamelan Music
Indian Raga
African Drumming
Music Drawing on Different Cultures

Area of Study 4: *Gamelan Music*
Langiang

as recorded by Sekehe Gender Bharata Muni, from the village of Sading, Bali

Balinese

Langiang is a piece for Gamelan *Gender Wayang*, an ensemble that accompanies performances of *Wayang Kulit Parwa*, shadow puppet plays that tell stories from the Hindu epic *Mahabharata*. This piece is played at the end of a night-time performance as the audience departs.

The ensemble comprises four Gender Wayang, each a two-octave metallophone with ten bronze keys suspended over bamboo tube resonators. Two instruments are tuned an octave higher than the other two. One gender of each pair is tuned slightly higher in pitch than its partner, so that acoustic 'beats' occur when they are played together.

Each player has two wooden beaters with disc-shaped heads. Usually the left hands play a basic melody in unison, while the right hands perform complex interlocking figuration (*kotekan*), consisting of two parts: *polos* ('plain') and *sangsih* ('differing').

The tuning is a pentatonic scale called *slendro*:
2 3 5 6 1 2 3 5 6 1̇ (low → high)

Dots below or above the numbers indicate pitches an octave lower or higher respectively. The notation uses lines above the numbers to group notes into faster, half-length pairs.

Approximate equivalent pitches: (musical staff showing pitches 1, 2, 3, 5, 6)

The piece *Langiang* is a series of melodic cells that alternate and modulate.

Time	Description
0'00"	The theme is stated at the beginning – the left hands, in the lower octave, play **A** 3[5 6 3 5 3 6 5 3] and the right hands play 3[5 6 3 5 3 6 5 3]. Played six times.
0'11"	The left hands shift up two notes to **B** 6[1 2 3 1 3 2 1 6] and the right hands continue as before. Played six times.
0'22"	Returns to **A**, six times more.
0'32"	Transition **T1** 6 5 3 5 3 2 and modulation. Both hands move down one note to **C**: left hands 2[3 5 2 3 2 5 3 2] and right hands 2[3 5 2 3 2 5 3 2] – played six times.
0'44"	Left hands shift up two notes to **D** 5[6 1 2 6 2 1 6 5] and right hands continue as before. Played six times.
0'54"	Returns to **C**, again six times. Notice that the sequence **C D C** is identical to the previous one (**A B A**), only a note lower.
1'05"	Another transition **T2** 5 · 6 5 3 and a modulation up one note, which takes the piece into its second phase, with a different scheme but similar modulation. The left hand theme **E** [· 5 · 6 5 3 2 5 6 · · 5 6 3 6 5 3] is played twice, while the right hand decorates using 3 5 6 3 5 6 3 etc.
1'21"	Transition **T1** occurs again, and both hands move down one note, i.e. left hand **F** [· 3 · 5 3 2 5 · · 3 5 2 5 3 2] which is played twice, with right hand 2 3 5 2 3 5 2 etc. Notice that **F** is identical to **E**, only a note lower.
1'38"	Transition **T2** again shifts the theme and decoration back up one note to **E**, which is played twice more.
1'54"	Transition **T1** shifts everything back down one note to **F**, played twice more.
2'11"	Transition **T2** occurs again, slowing down this time and ending on note 6 in a kind of resolution · 3 · 5 · 6 5 3 · 5 1 5 6

Area of Study 4: *Gamelan Music*

Jauk Masal

as recorded by Gong Kebyar of Sebatu, Bali.

Balinese

'Jauk' is a Balinese masked dance depicting demons. The dancers, usually male, wear elaborate conical headdresses, masks with large bulging eyes, and white gloves with long fingernails.

Instruments:

All metallophones are tuned in pairs to create acoustic 'beatings'

Gong – large hanging gong (ends every cycle)
Kempur – smaller hanging gong
Kemong – smallest hanging gong (bisects each cycle)
Kempli – small horizontally mounted gong (keeps the pulse)
Jegogan – pair of largest one-octave metallophones
Calung – pair of smaller one-octave metallophones
Ugal – largest two-octave metallophone (melodic leader)
Gangsa: Pemade – two pairs of smaller two-octave metallophones
Kantilan – two pairs of smallest two-ocatve metallophones
Reyong – row of 12 horizontally mounted gong chimes played by four players
Kendang – two-headed drum
Ceng-Ceng – small horizontally mounted cymbals
Suling – bamboo flutes

The tuning is a pentatonic scale called *pelog.*

Approximate equivalent pitches:

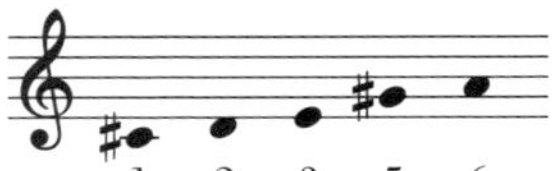

1 2 3 5 6

Angsel: a melodic/rhythmic break cued by the dancers via a drum signal

Pokok (trunk melody):

Kempli +
Kemong ^
Kempur v
Gong ○

```
+ [ +   +   +   +   +   +   +   +   +   +   +   +   +   +   +   +  ]
                                ^       v               v
(6)[    1       6       1       2       5       3       1      (6) ]
```

The Gamelan Gong Kebyar

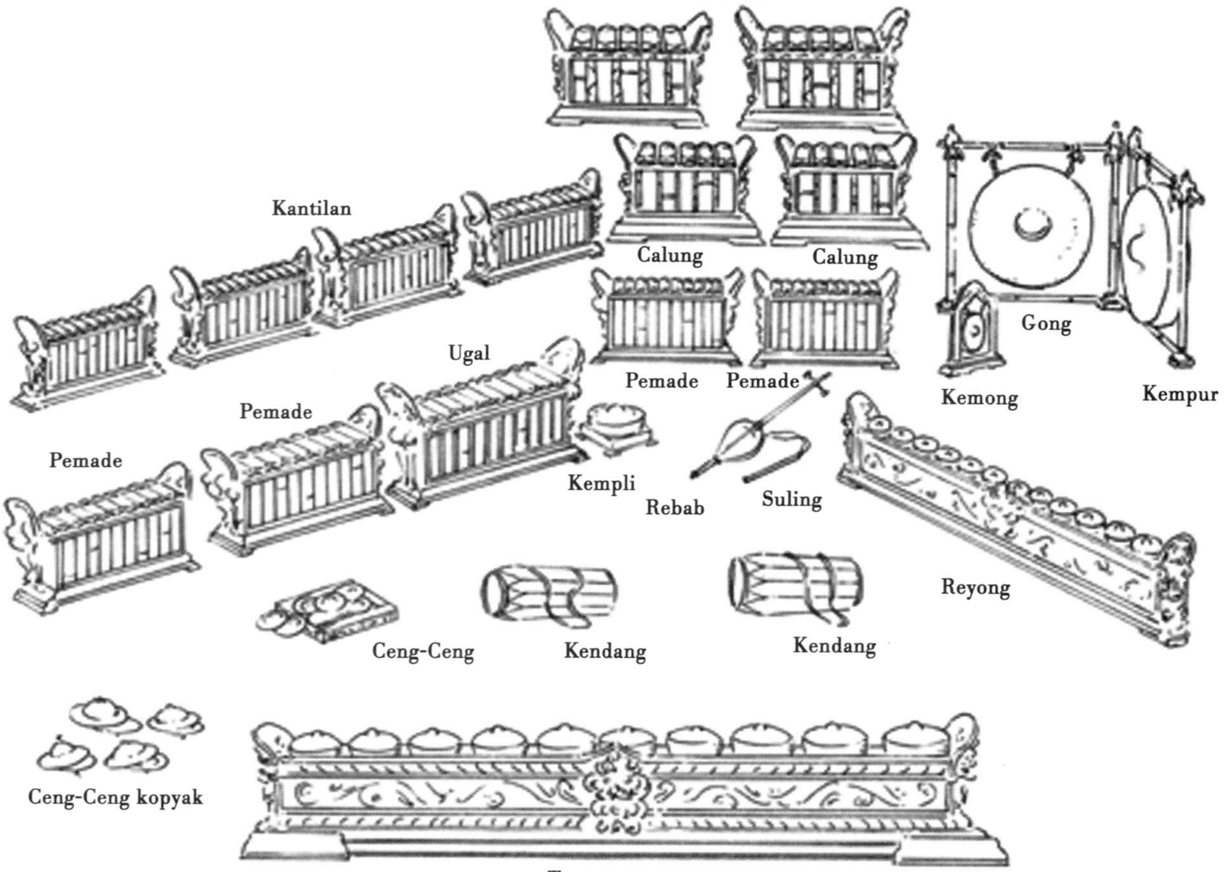
Jegogang
Kantilan
Calung
Calung
Gong
Ugal
Pemade
Pemade
Pemade
Pemade
Kemong
Kempur
Kempli
Rebab
Suling
Reyong
Ceng-Ceng
Kendang
Kendang
Ceng-Ceng kopyak
Trompong

Time-line
(⊕ indicates gong)

Time	Gong	Event
0′00″	−	Ugal introduction and drum
07″	⊕	First gong: pokok (core melody) and kempli (pulse) start
12″	−	Drum signal
13″	⊕	Rest of gamelan enter loud (reyong offbeat pattern)
	⊕	
24″	−	Angsel (melodic/rhythmic break)
28″	−	Reyong kotekan (melodic pattern)
	⊕	*Dancers enter ('malpal')*
	⊕	*– movements tense*
	⊕	*Kempli speed ~160*
	⊕	
54″	⊕	Drum signal → loud
58″	−	Angsel
	⊕	
	⊕	
1′20″	⊕	Drum signal → loud
1′24″	−	Angsel
	⊕	
	⊕	
1′47″	⊕	Drum signal → loud → angsel
1′52″	⊕	Long angsel: fast/loud (series of climaxes/breaks)
	⊕	
2′06″	−	End of angsel
2′11″	⊕	Gamelan re-enters: strong, sustained
	⊕	
	⊕	
	⊕	
2′31″	⊕	Drum signal → loud
2′35″	−	Angsel
	⊕	
	⊕	
2′57″	⊕	Drum signal → loud → angsel
3′02″	⊕	Long angsel: fast/loud
	⊕	
3′16″	⊕	End of angsel
3′20″	⊕	Gamelan re-enters: strong, sustained
	⊕	
	⊕	
	⊕	
3′40″	⊕	Drum signal → loud → angsel
3′45″	⊕	Long angsel: fast/loud
	⊕	
3′55″	−	End of angsel
3′56″	⊕	Drum signal → second section of piece 'pengipuk' (kempli suddenly half previous rate)
4′02″	−	Angsel
4′03″		Strong, slowing down *Dancers' movements*
		more expansive
4′11″	−	Angsel
4′12″	⊕	Slower, softer from gong *(Kempli speed ~48)*
4′23″	−	Kemong
4′34″	⊕	Drum signal → faster/louder
4′41″	−	Angsel
4′43″		Strong
4′52″	−	Angsel
4′53″	⊕	Slower, softer from gong
5′03″	−	Kemong
5′13″	⊕	Drum signal → faster/louder, speeding up
5′20″	−	Angsel
5′21″		Strong, speeding up more
5′27″	⊕	Return to first section of piece, speeding up (reyong offbeat pattern)
5′30″	−	Drum signal → loud
5′33″	⊕	Long angsel: fast/loud *Dancers: tense movements*
		(as before)
	⊕	*Kempli ~ 160*
5′44″	−	End of angsel
5′45″	⊕	More relaxed
5′47″	−	Reyong kotekan
	⊕	
	⊕	
	⊕	
6′13″	⊕	Drum signal → loud
6′18″	⊕	Long angsel: fast/loud
	⊕	
6′29″	−	End of angsel → drum signal
6′30″	⊕	Slowing down to end
6′39″	⊕	Final gong

Area of Study 4: *Indian Raga*

Rag Durga

as recorded by Shruti Sadolikar Katkar (vocal) with Madhukar Kothare (tabla)

North Indian

In Hindu mythology Durga is an all-powerful goddess, who defeated an army of demons and saved the universe. She was as beautiful as she was deadly and is often portrayed as a goddess with an attractive and gentle face. The mood associated with raga Durga is pleasant and philosophical. Ragas have a favoured time for performance; Durga is intended as a late-night raga.

A raga is a pattern of notes which is a cross between a scale and a melody. Here is the ascending and descending form of raga Durga (in many ragas these forms differ, but in this case they are the same):

The names of the scale notes are: *sa, re, ga, ma, pa, dha, ni, sa*. These are often abbreviated to *S R G M P D N S* as in these examples. A dot above the note shows that it is an octave higher, a dot below means that it is an octave lower. Here is the melodic outline of raga Durga:

We hear first the drone instrument, a tanpura. Then the singer begins the *alap* (slow introduction), echoed in the background by a sarangi (a bowed string instrument):

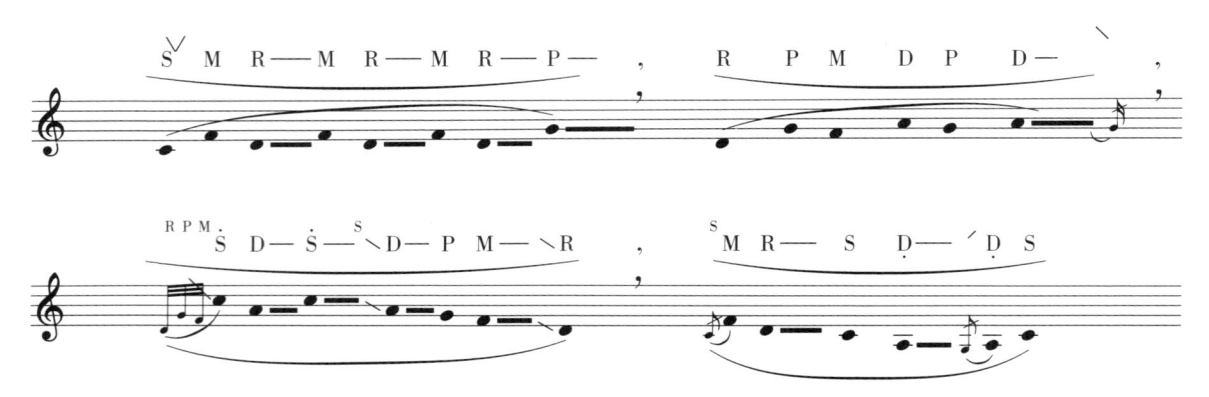

At 0′40″, where the 'composition' begins, the tabla (a pair of hand drums) join in:

चतुर सुघरा आवो रे	Come clever beautiful one
बालमवा ले हो कन्हैया ।	Oh my darling Kanhaiya
बहुत दिनन में मिलन भयो है	We are meeting after many days
काहे अब लो तोरा ॥	Well, now take what is yours, you clever beautiful one.

[Kanhaiya is another name for the Hindu god Krishna]

Each raga uses a rhythmic cycle known as a tala. The most popular tala is *tintal*, and it is used in raga Durga. The cycle has 16 beats divided into four groups of four. You can hear the *tintal* played on the tabla.

Area of Study 4: *Indian Raga*
Rag Brindabani Sarang
as recorded by Buddhadev DasGupta (sarod) with Devendra Kanti Chakrabarty (tabla)

North Indian

This example of north Indian classical music presents many of the key features of a full raga performance, but in a condensed form: the full version would last at least 45 minutes in total (including sections such as *jor* and *jhala*, which are omitted here). It is performed by Buddhadev DasGupta on sarod – a kind of lute with no frets but with a polished metal fingerboard. He is accompanied by Devendra Kanti Chakrabarty on the tabla, a pair of drums played with the hands (i.e. without sticks). You will also hear the tanpura, another type of lute, playing a drone: a repeated pattern, emphasizing the key note, *Sa*. The tanpura is most noticeable in the first few seconds, before the sarod begins, and also between the two 'compositions' (see below).

There are three main phases in the performance: an unmetered solo introduction (called *alap*) played on the sarod; followed by two sections each based on a different composition (*gat*), one slow and the other fast. Both of the *gat* sections are accompanied by the tabla. The slow composition is set to a metre called *dhamar tal*, comprising 14 beats (each 14-beat pattern lasts a little over 9 seconds). The faster piece is in *tintal*, of 16 beats (the pattern lasts between 3 and 4 seconds). DasGupta plays the compositions, and also demonstrates some of the most common ways of improvising. Chakrabarty plays a basic tabla pattern (called *theka*) most of the time, but also plays a few short solos.

The piece is set in a raga called Brindabani Sarang (the name refers to Brindaban, a town in northern India strongly associated with Lord Krishna.) It is classified as pentatonic, but one of the five notes occurs in two forms, notated here as B♭ and B. In general, the B is used when the melody is ascending, the B♭ when it is descending.

Time	Description
0′01″	The tanpura begins the drone.
0′05″	Buddhadev DasGupta begins to play the *alap* on the sarod. You may notice in particular the sliding effects, called *meend*, which are produced by the soloist sliding his finger along the metal fingerboard after the string has been plucked; since there are no frets, each slide is continuous.
1′17″	DasGupta begins to play the first composition or *gat*. When he reaches the *sam*, the first beat of the metre, the tabla joins in (1′ 19″). This piece is in *dhamar tal*: it should be possible to count 14 beats from one *sam* to the next (once the tabla gets going properly, we generally hear one drum-stroke per beat). *Sam* arrives on 1′19″, 1′29″, 1′38″, 1′47″, 1′57″, and so on.
1′43″	Having completed the *gat* itself, DasGupta starts to improvise. This improvisation sometimes comprises rapid runs up and down the scale, called *tans*.
1′52″–1′57″	From time to time the tabla player takes centre stage, playing his own flourishes while the sarod just repeats the *gat*. This is the first of these episodes and, as we would expect, it ends on *sam*.
2′18″	The soloist resumes his improvisation. In this passage we also hear a couple of *tihais*: a *tihai* is a phrase or pattern repeated three times, usually arranged so as to end on *sam*. Tihais here end on *sam* at 3′01″ and 3′27″.
3′37″	The *dhamar tal* section ends.
3′41″	The second *gat* now begins. This composition is set in *tintal*, a pattern of 16 beats; again the basic tabla pattern has one stroke per beat. The tabla joins in on *sam*, at 3′45″. This section of the *gat* extends over two cycles of *tintal*, and is repeated. Then DasGupta plays the second section of the *gat*, again stretching over two cycles of the tal, and followed by a return to the first section.
	In detail:
3′41″–3′49″	first section of the *gat* (two cycles)
3′49″–3′57″	first section repeated (two cycles)
3′57″–4′05″	second section (two cycles)
4′05″–4′09″	beginning of first section repeated
c. 4′15″	After this repetition, the soloist begins to improvise. Once again we hear sequences of *tans*, interspersed with *tihais* (e.g. arriving at *sam* at 5′07″) and a short tabla solo near the end of the performance (5′18″).

Area of Study 4: *African Drumming*

Kundum

as recorded by drummers of Ghana

Ghanaian

Kundum is a harvest festival of the Ahanta people who live in an area along the coast of Ghana. The six-week period of the festival begins around June. Much drumming, singing, dancing, and eating of new yams takes place during this time. The master drum in each community announces the beginning of the festival; in addition it may be carried with shoulder straps and played in a festival procession. The highlight of the Kundum festival is the four days in the middle of this six-week period. Musical performances on these particular days start in the afternoon and last until late evening or even longer.

Drummers come together before the festival to form a temporary band known as *ebise*. Three weeks before the festival, practice sessions are held where boys and men are given opportunities to play along with experienced musicians. If they become good enough, they are given a chance to play publicly during the festival.

Unaccompanied *ebise* songs alternate with intense periods of drumming and dancing. The dancers wear ankle rattles of eyisen seeds, and may punctuate the drumming with rhythmic riffs on police whistles.

The master drum is *kundum kenle*, a tall drum that rests on the ground, tilting forward. The right hand holds the stick, while the left hand mutes the drumhead and strikes notes. The *dawuro*, a bell, is used to provide the time-line along with a *ntroa* rattle, i.e. a gourd or cigarette tin filled with seeds or gravel. The *operenten* drum is bottle shaped and is held between the knees while the performer is sitting.

There are two dances – slow and fast – at the Kundum festival, each with its corresponding drum patterns. On the recording the fast dance immediately follows the slow dance.

Slow Kundum
This opens with introductory solo phrases by the master drummer.
The time-line is heard on the *dawuro*:

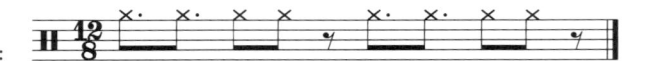

The *kagan* drum can also be heard underlining the rhythm:

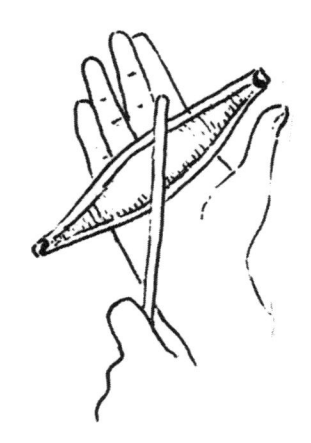

Dawuro

A noticeable feature of this dance is the way in which duple and triple rhythms are played simultaneously. The bell part alternates two even beats with three even beats, whilst the *kagan* always plays three. This gives the master drummer considerable scope to vary his phrases between these two 'feels'.

When the whole group is cued in, the master drummer improvises using mainly traditional patterns. The low note is the normal sound of the drum when hit by a stick and the high sound is achieved by using the other hand to press down on the skin of the drum. Here are some of the one-bar rhythms used by the master drummer on Slow Kundum.

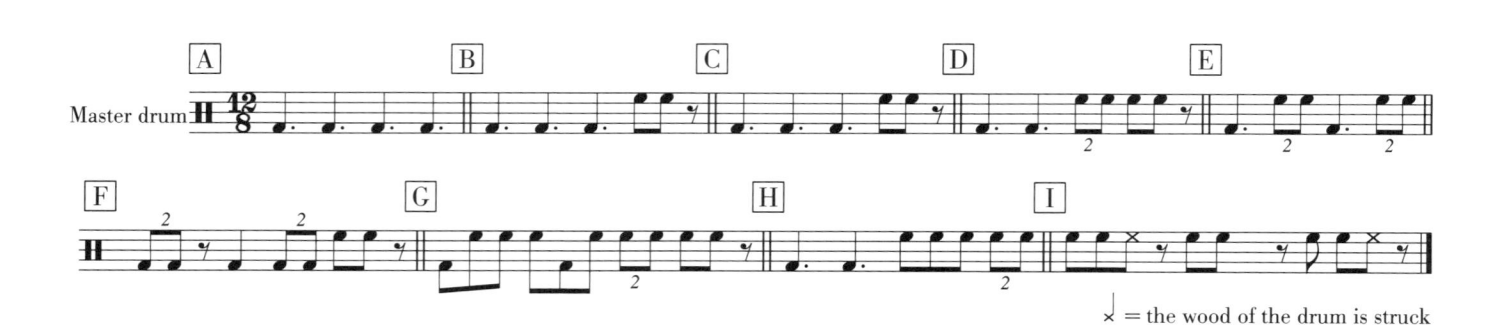

Master drum

× = the wood of the drum is struck

Fast Kundum

Here is the time-line and the underlying rhythms of the fast section. The time-line can be clearly heard.

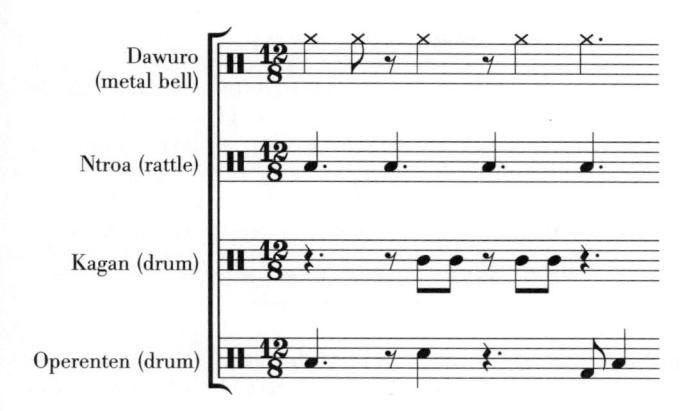

Dawuro (metal bell)
Ntroa (rattle)
Kagan (drum)
Operenten (drum)

Here are some of the one- and two-bar rhythms used by the master drummer on Fast Kundum.

Kagan

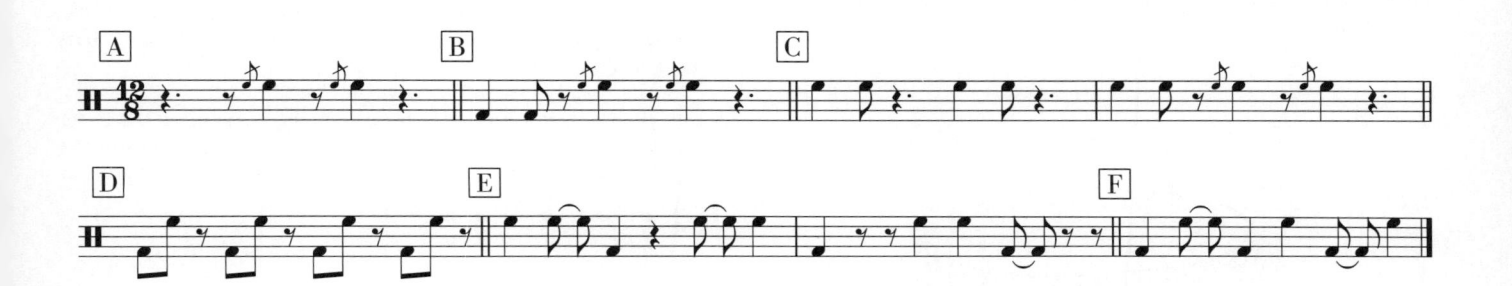

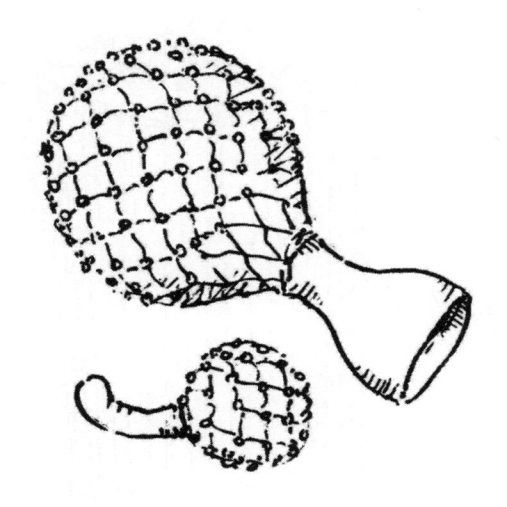

Ntroa

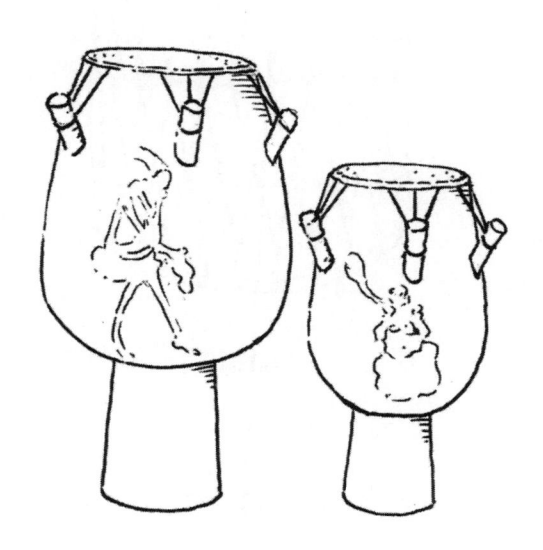

Petia and Operenten

125

Area of Study 4: *African Drumming*

Nzekele

as recorded by Les Percussions de Guinée

Guinean

The Transcription

African drumming is not normally written down. Transcriptions of world music often lack the subtlety and freedom that exist in the music, rounding rhythms up to values that are easier to notate. If a rhythm is not played quite in time to our ears, we should remember that in many musical styles around the world this is an entirely acceptable practice. A good example of this 'looseness' in the playing is at letter C (page 128) where the figure is not always played strictly 'in time' as it is passed around the group. When transcribed into Western staff notation, *Nzekele* looks very complex. Listen out for the unison riffs to help you follow the music.

The following transcription does not specify all the instruments used; and each rhythm may be played by more than one person. The score should be considered, then, as a rhythmic map of the piece. Where possible, it places parts in relation to each other – low at the bottom of the score, high at the top. The two lowest drums are the *sangban* and the *dundun*.

Drums vary a lot in the length that they sustain after being struck. To get round this problem when notating percussion music, a smaller note-length is often written even though the actual note may last much longer. So it has to be remembered that a quaver on a low drum will not sound the same length as a quaver on a high drum, or metal bell!

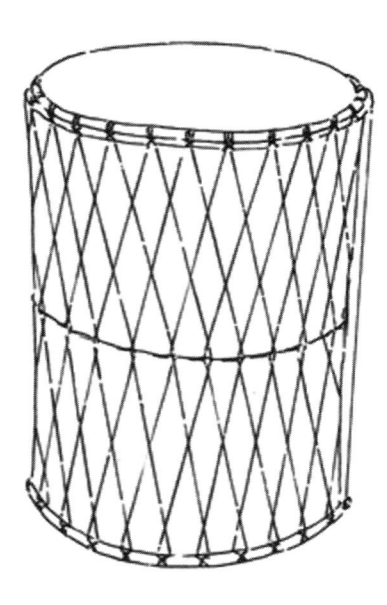

Nzekele

The piece opens with an introductory solo. (A series of virtuosic, flamboyant gestures is often used as a sort of fanfare to get the attention of musicians and dancers as well as giving expressive freedom to the soloist.)

The rhythm that is used at letter A is based on the following syncopated phrase:

This rhythm is frequently heard in African music and music which has an African influence (e.g. Cuban). It can be heard in many styles of music around the world.

At letter B you will here a drum cue. The system of cueing the entire group is an example of 'call and response'. The cue may be a recognizable rhythm that is played the same each time, or it may be accompanied by a visual signal.

The first main section has a time signature that is very common in West African drumming, having 12 units divided into four main beats. The way in which the bass drums share a sort of melodic pattern between them is a good example of **hocketing**. Notice also the unison rhythmic 'chorus' alternating with other patterns. These other patterns are not always the same length (many are three bars instead of two).

A roll (the Western term for a drum tremolo) announces the faster (second) section, which features extended solos by members of the group. Here the rhythm is based on the following syncopated phrase:

This rhythm is more famous as **clave**, the foundation of much Cuban music. It originated in African music and was taken to Cuba by slaves.

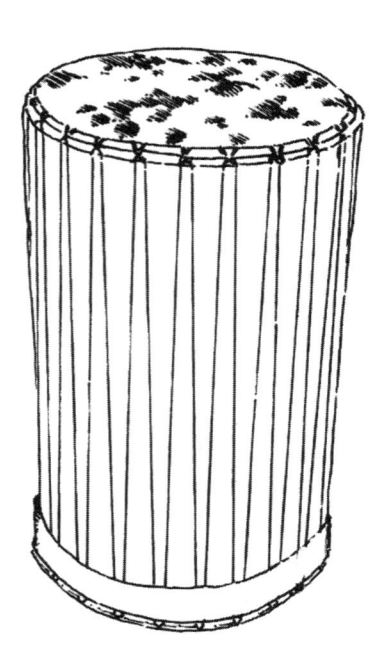

DunDun

Sangban

127

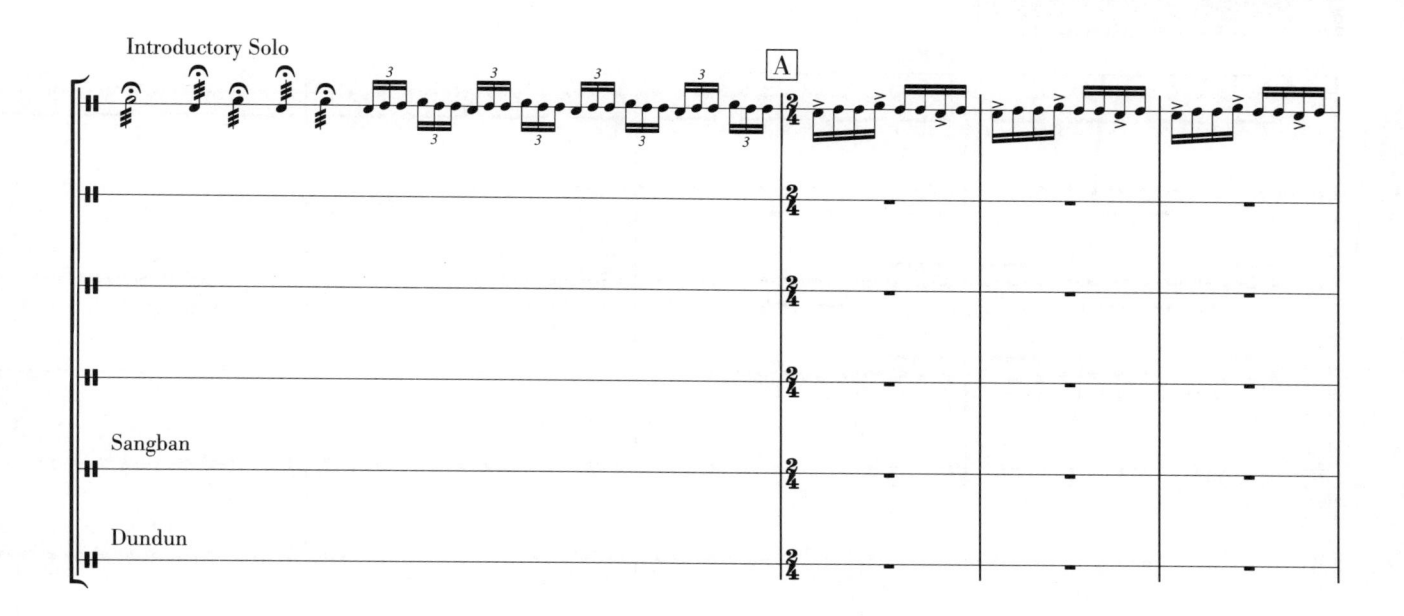

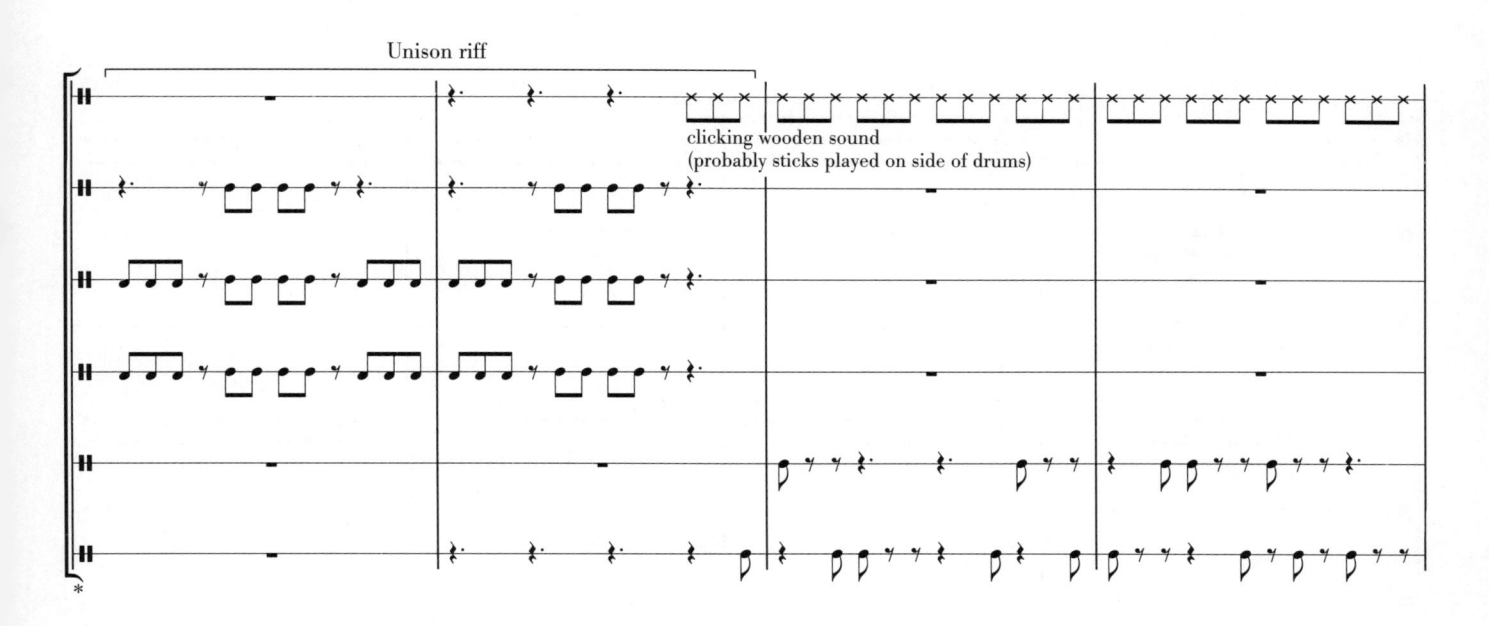

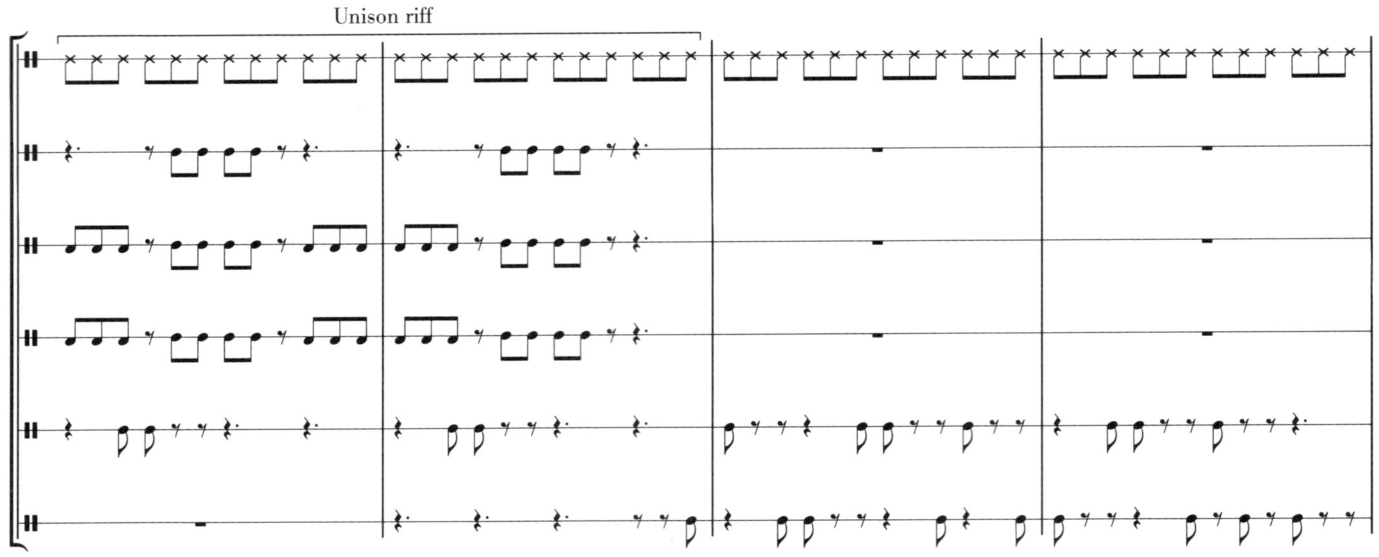
Unison riff

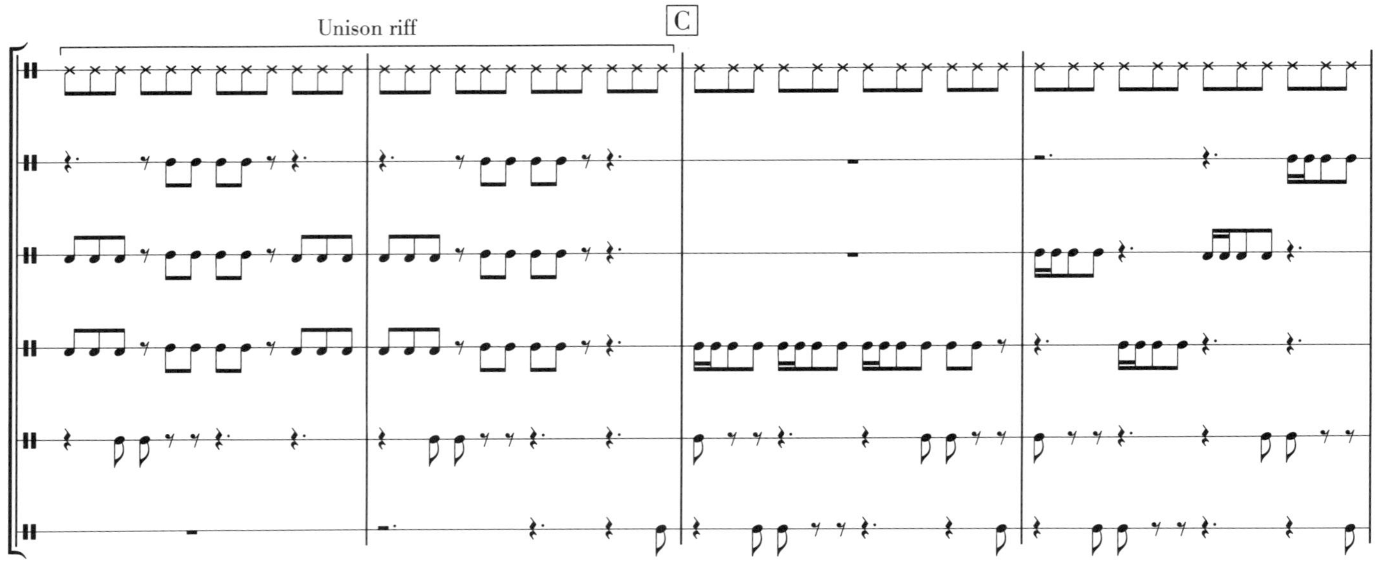
Unison riff
C

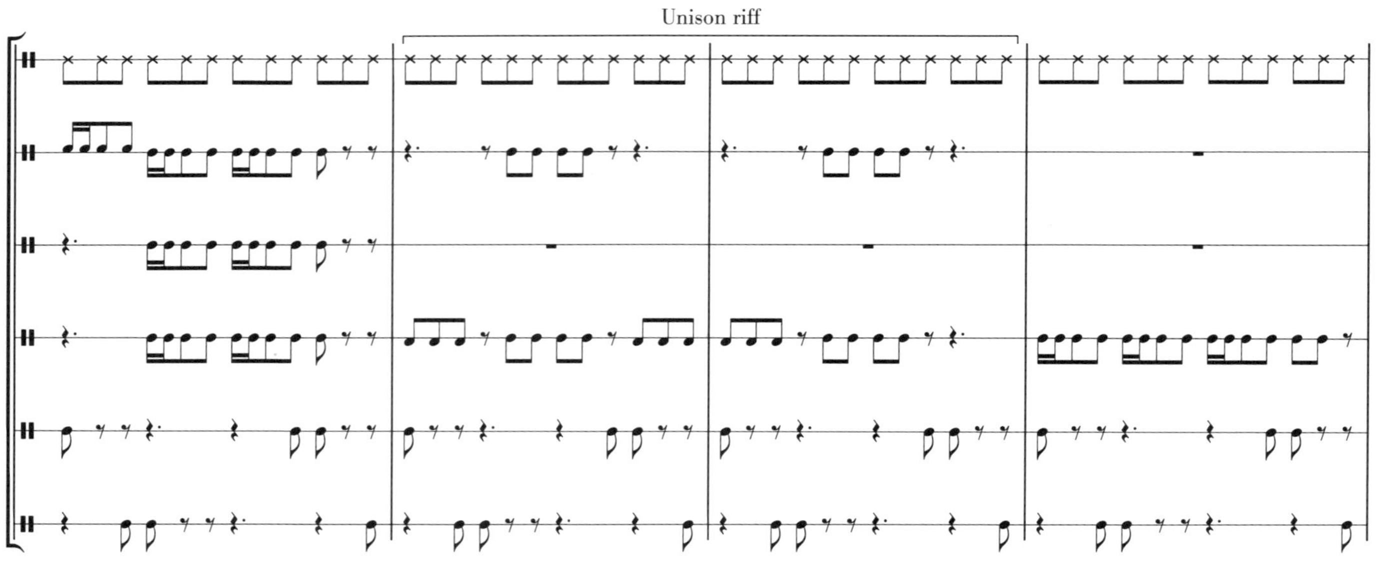
Unison riff

129

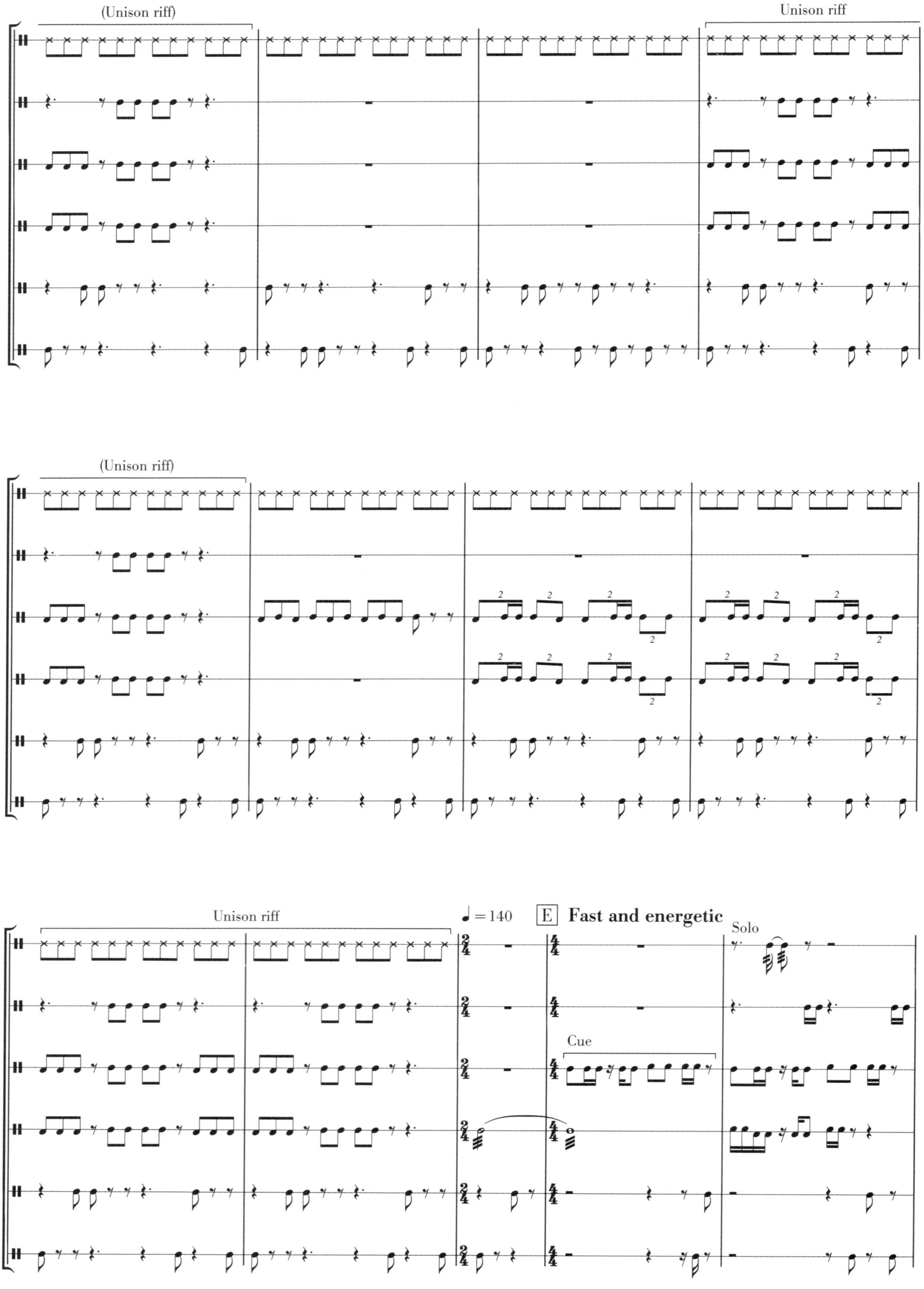
(Unison riff)
Unison riff
(Unison riff)
Unison riff
♩ = 140
E
Fast and energetic
Solo
Cue

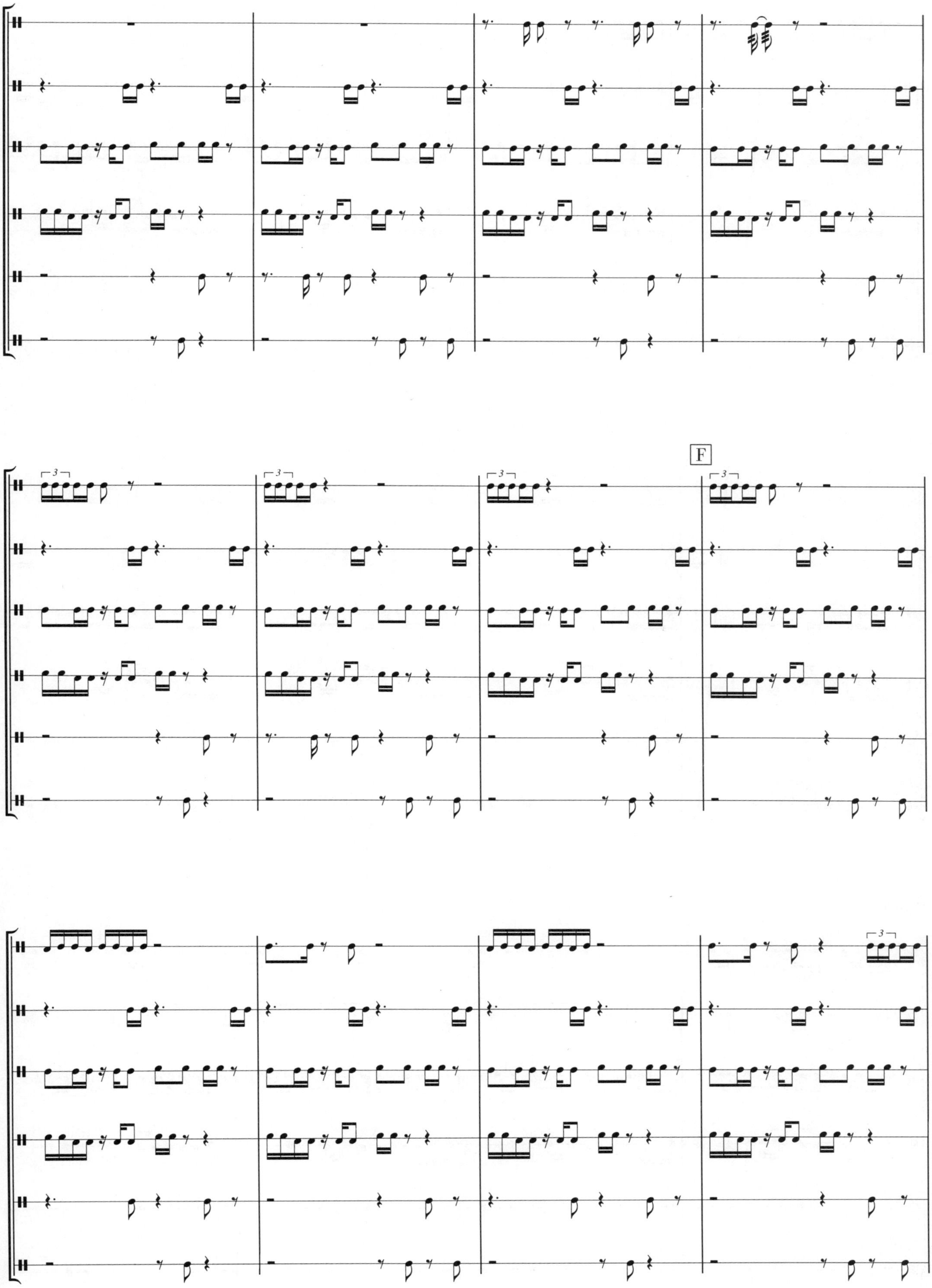
F

etc.

Area of Study 4: *Music Drawing on Different Cultures*
Suite for Violin, Piano and Small Orchestra: Second Gamelan

Lou Harrison
(b. 1917)

One of the instruments used in this piece is the Tack Piano – an upright piano with thumb tacks (or drawing pins) inserted into the hammers to produce a percussive, metallic sound. Lou Harrison invented this in 1941.

134

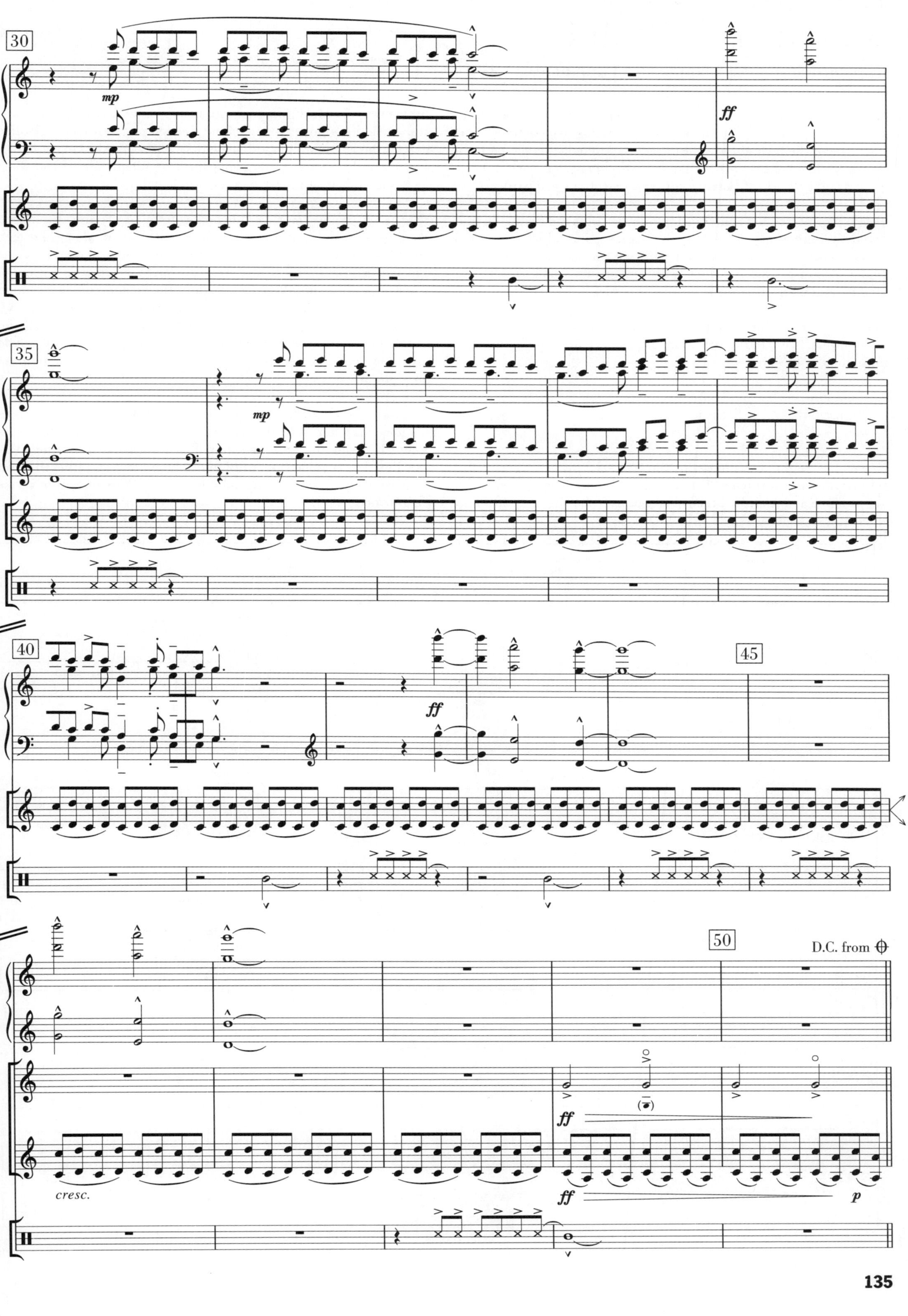

30
mp
ff
35
mp
40
ff
45
50
D.C. from ⊕
cresc.
ff
(𝅗𝅥)
ff
p

Area of Study 4: *Music Drawing on Different Cultures*

Mundian To Bach Ke

as recorded by Labh Janjua and Panjabi MC, 1998

Panjabi MC

Bhangra is a lively form of folk music and dance originating from Punjab. It is normally accompanied by singing (*boliyaan* – short poems) and the beat of the *dohl* drum. Traditionally people perform bhangra when celebrating the harvest. Now bhangra is performed in all parts of the world at Indian weddings, receptions and parties.

This bhanga track has quite a simple form. After the mandolin and percussion introduction, we hear the main section, which comprises a first verse, a chorus, a second verse and a bridge passage. The whole section is then repeated (with only a very small variation in length), and then a brief coda finishes the track.

Mundian To Bach Ke is built up in layers and blocks. There are five main layers, which use the same repeated (or looped) material throughout. They are:

1. Mandolins   4. Drum machine
2. Percussion   5. Electric bass
3. Voice

Listen for slight variations in the material, especially in the percussion and vocal parts. The percussionists use complex patterns to introduce and round off their material, and the singer's vocal line changes with each verse.

In this song, layers are formed into blocks of two, four or eight bars, and are added gradually throughout the first part of the track. Notice that all the layers are heard for the first time when the singer arrives at the vocal chorus, emphasizing the words and title of the song. Layers are taken away and then re-introduced.

The track mixes musical elements from Asia and the West. Traditional and electronic instruments are heard alongside each other, as are different systems of rhythm and pitch. While the voice and electric bass tend to use 'regular' Western pitching (although according to a non-Western mode), the mandolins are tuned differently: their part features a F quartertone flat (notated as ♩), which is sharper than a E but flatter than a F. And although the mandolins, percussion and vocals are delivered with a swing-type rhythmic feel, the drum machine and bass play even quavers throughout.

Mundian To Bach Ke was released around the time of Busta Rhymes's rap hit 'Fire it Up'. The track makes reference to that record by using the bass line from Busta Rhymes's recording. The bass line (and a guitar and synth line, which are both rather difficult to hear on this track) is originally from the 1980s television series *Knightrider*.

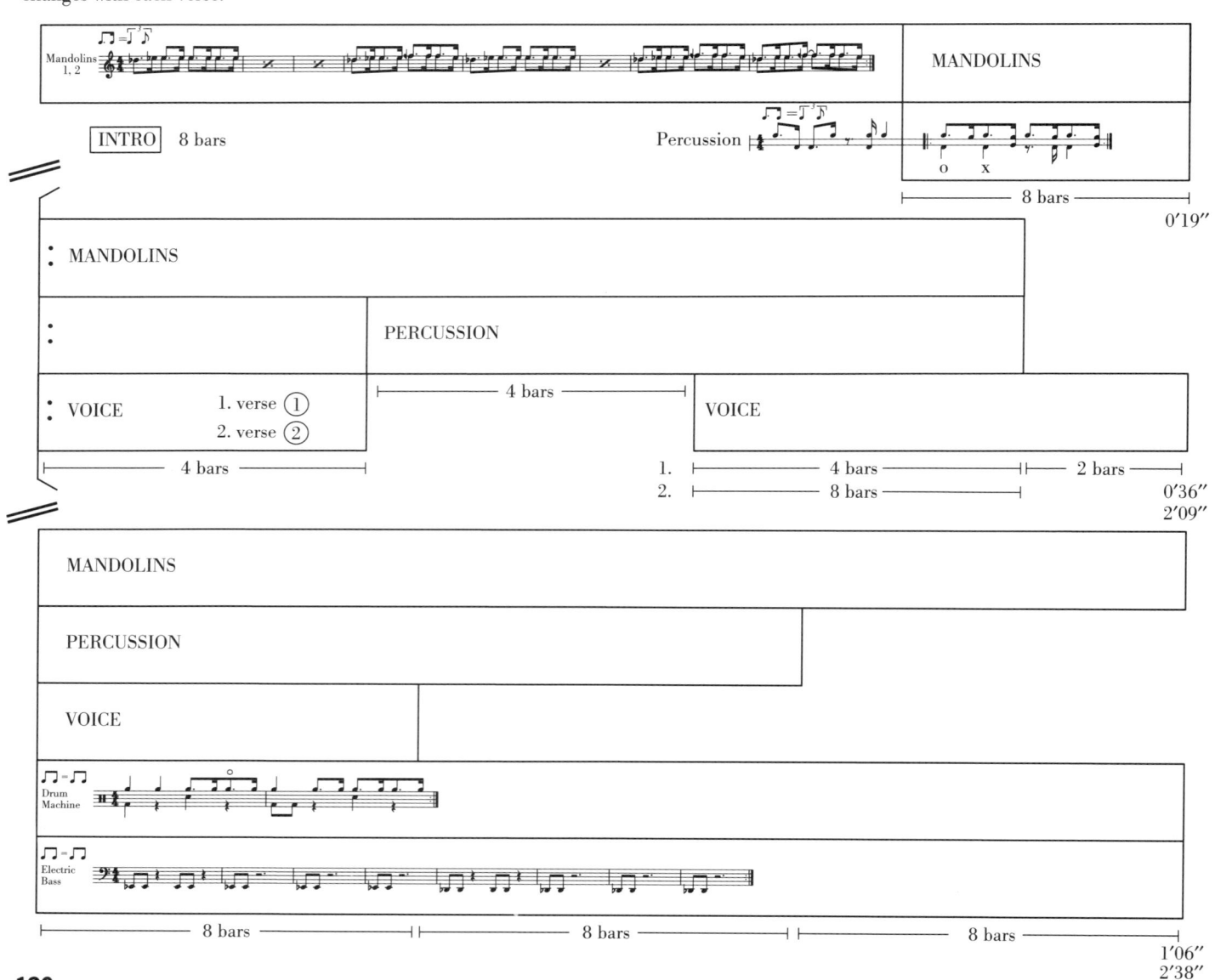

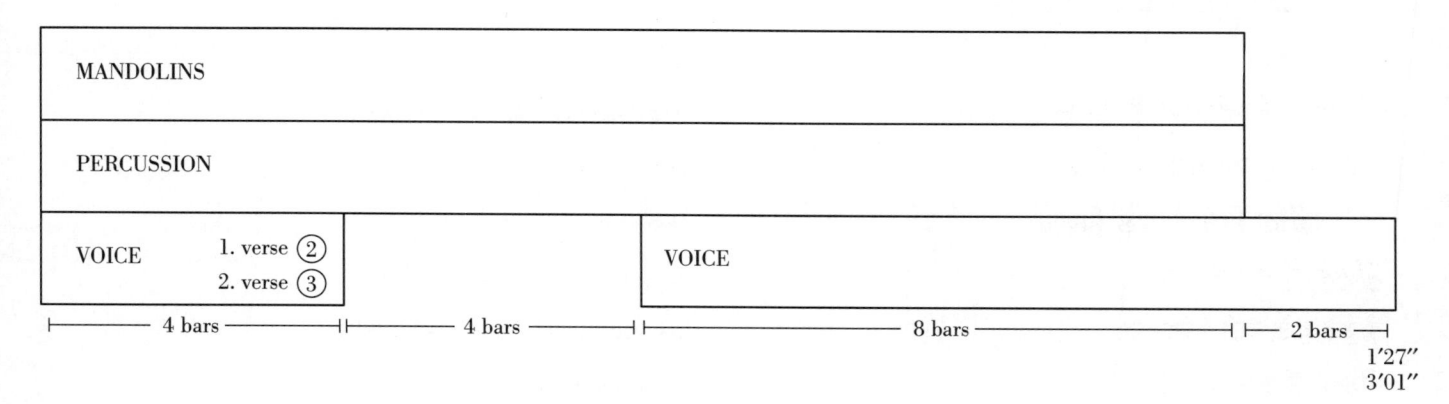

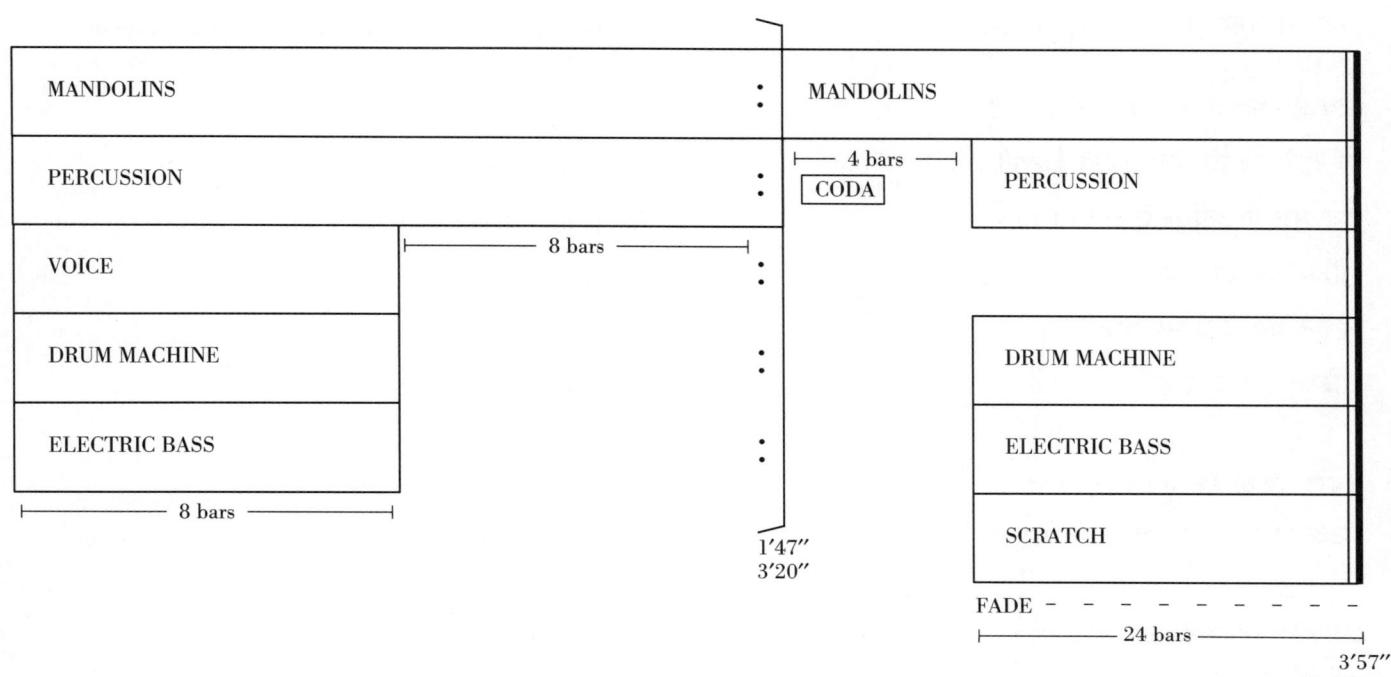

Vocals

Verse ①

ਨੀਂਮੀਆਂ ਤੋਂ ਬੁੱਝਦੀ ਰੁਕਾ ਕੇ ਰੱਖ ਲੈ	(O maiden) Let your flame not dim
ਪੱਲੇ ਵਿਚ ਮੁਖੜਾ ਲੁਕਾ ਕੇ ਰੱਖ ਲੈ	Hide your face in the veil
ਐਵੇਂ ਕਰੀਂ ਨਾ ਕਿਸੇ ਦੇ ਨਾਲ ਪਿਆਰ	Don't fall in love unwisely
ਮੁੰਡਿਆਂ ਤੋਂ ਬਚ ਕੇ ਰਹੀਂ	Keep away from boys
ਤੂੰ ਹੁਣੇ ਹੁਣੇ ਹੋਈ ਮੁਟਿਆਰ	You have just blossomed as a maiden
ਮੁੰਡਿਆਂ ਤੋਂ ਬਚ ਕੇ ਰਹੀਂ	Keep away from boys.
ਤੇਰਾ ਕੀ ਕਸੂਰ ਜੇ ਨਸ਼ੀਲੇ ਨੈਣ ਹੋ ਗਏ	Why blame yourself as your eyes have become intoxicating
ਦੇਖ ਕੇ ਅਦਾਵਾਂ ਸ਼ਰਮੀਲੇ ਨੈਣ ਹੋ ਗਏ	And shy as you make amorous gestures
ਸਾਂਭ ਕੇ ਰੱਖ ਨੀ ਇਹ ਜੋਬਨੀ ਪਟਾਰੀ	Preserve your basket of youth
ਹੁਣ ਮੁੜ ਕੇ ਨਹੀਂ ਆਉਣੀ ਇਹ ਬਹਾਰ	This spring will never come again
ਮੁੰਡਿਆਂ ਤੋਂ ਬਚ ਕੇ ਰਹੀਂ	Keep away from boys
ਤੂੰ ਹੁਣੇ ਹੁਣੇ ਹੋਈ ਮੁਟਿਆਰ	You have just blossomed as a maiden
ਮੁੰਡਿਆਂ ਤੋਂ ਬਚ ਕੇ ਰਹੀਂ	Keep away from boys.
ਚੜ੍ਹਦੀ ਜਵਾਨੀ ਤੇਰਾ ਰੂਪ ਦਾ ਸੰਵਾਰਦਾ	Early youth makes you more charming
ਪਤਲਾ ਜਿਹਾ ਲੱਕ ਨਾ ਹੁਲਾਰਾ ਨੀ ਸਹਾਰਦਾ	Your tender waist is unable to bear your swinging movement
ਗੋਰਾ ਗੋਰਾ ਰੰਗ ਉੱਤੋਂ ਮੇਰੀ ਗਾਨੀ ਤੁੱਲ	Your fair colour is fairer than gold
ਨਹੀਂ ਤੇਰੇ ਜਿਹੀ ਸੋਹਣੀ ਕੋਈ ਨਾਰ	There is none more beautiful than you
ਮੁੰਡਿਆਂ ਤੋਂ ਬਚ ਕੇ ਰਹੀਂ	Keep away from boys
ਤੂੰ ਹੁਣੇ ਹੁਣੇ ਹੋਈ ਮੁਟਿਆਰ	You have just blossomed as a maiden
ਮੁੰਡਿਆਂ ਤੋਂ ਬਚ ਕੇ ਰਹੀਂ	Keep away from boys.
ਮੁੰਡਿਆਂ ਦੇ ਬੁੱਲ੍ਹਾਂ ਉੱਤੇ ਤੇਰੀਆਂ ਕਹਾਣੀਆਂ	Boys keep talking about you
ਚੰਨੀ ਨੇ ਤੇ ਗੌਣੇ ਦੀਆਂ ਗਲੀਆਂ ਪਛਾਣੀਆਂ	Channi even knows the routes you take
ਜੰਜੂਆ ਤਾਂ ਹੋਇਆ ਤੇਰੇ ਰੂਪ ਦਾ ਦੀਵਾਨਾ	'Janjua' is mad after you
ਐਵੇਂ ਡੱਕਿਆ ਨਾ ਹੁਸਨ ਦਬਾ	Why keep your beauty suppressed
ਮੁੰਡਿਆਂ ਤੋਂ ਬਚ ਕੇ ਰਹੀਂ	Keep away from boys
ਤੂੰ ਹੁਣੇ ਹੁਣੇ ਹੋਈ ਮੁਟਿਆਰ	You have just blossomed as a maiden
ਮੁੰਡਿਆਂ ਤੋਂ ਬਚ ਕੇ ਰਹੀਂ ।	Keep away from boys.

Questions

The majority of these questions can be answered just by listening, i.e. without the score; others are more suitable for use with the score. For each piece of music there are questions to cover a wide range of ability. In some cases these questions overlap; they are not necessarily intended to be used at the same time.

The questions are designed to provide classroom listening activities rather than to act as a blueprint for future examination papers.

Generic Questions

The following questions can be adapted to fit many of the extracts:

1. How would you describe the music of this opening section?
2. Is the piece in a major or minor key?
3. What key is this piece in?
4. How many beats are there in each bar?
5. What type of cadence does the piece end with?
6. Is the texture homophonic, monophonic or polyphonic?
7. How would you describe the texture of this music?
8. Name FOUR instruments that you can hear.
9. Name the instrument (or instruments) playing the bass line.
10. Which family of instruments does this (or these) instrument(s) belong to?
11. Name the solo instrument(s) heard.
12. Name an Italian term to describe the speed (or tempo) of this piece.
13. Describe the dynamics of this piece.
14. What dynamic marking would you give for the opening of this piece?
15. When was this piece composed?
16. Describe the mood of this music. How do the musical elements combine to create this mood or atmosphere?
17. How does the music reflect the words?
18. What are the main musical characteristics of this style of music (e.g. reggae, minimalism)?
19. What are the main features of this form (e.g. variations or rondo)?
20. Compare two pieces or extracts. Which do you prefer? Give TWO reasons why.
21. Write a short programme note for this piece of music.

Area of Study 1

Ground Bass

Purcell: 'Here the deities approve' from *Welcome to all the Pleasures*

1. What is a 'ground bass'?

2. Which of the following three statements is true of this song by Purcell:

    A The ground bass moves wholly in leaps.
    B The ground bass moves wholly in steps.
    C The ground bass moves by a mixture of leaps and steps.

3. Does the bass line change during the song?

4. In the extract that you are listening to, how many times is the ground bass heard?

5. Describe THREE ways in which Purcell introduces variety to the music with each repetition of the ground bass.

6. The piece ends with a purely instrumental passage where three solo instruments enter. Which of the following can you hear:

    A a violin, a guitar and a cello
    B two violas and a double bass
    C two violins and a viola

7. Name an ornament that is used in this piece.

8. Look at the score and name the three clefs found in this piece.

Marais: *Sonnerie de Ste Geneviève du mont de Paris*

1. Which of the following is played as the ground bass throughout the piece?

2. How many times do you hear this ground bass before the solo violin enters at the beginning of the piece?

3. The ground bass is repeated many times. Describe THREE ways in which the composer achieves variety.

Martland: Re-mix

1. Steve Martland's *Re-mix* and Marais' *Sonnerie de Ste Geneviève du mont de Paris* share the same musical material. Outline TWO similarities and TWO differences between the pieces.

2. These two pieces were written approximately 300 years apart. Name THREE features characteristic of twentieth-century music that can be heard in *Re-mix*.

3. Name TWO jazz techniques used by Martland in *Re-mix*.

Variations

Beethoven: Thirty-three Variations on a Waltz by Diabelli (theme and variations 1–4)

1. Choose THREE terms from those below which best describe the theme.

   simple triple   simple compound   dissonant
   sequential   vivace   adagio

2. Which of these three statements accurately describes the harmony of the theme:

   A It opens in the tonic major, modulates to the relative minor and returns to the tonic.
   B It opens in the tonic major, modulates to the dominant and returns to the tonic.
   C It opens in the tonic minor, modulates to the relative major and returns to the tonic.

3. Listen to Variation I, Variation II and Variation III. Choose TWO items from the list below to describe the musical characteristics of each variation:

   (a) lyrical
   (b) staccato
   (c) counterpoint
   (d) harmony
   (e) homophonic
   (f) same rhythm throughout

4. Which of these variations do you find most musically interesting? Why?

Paganini: Twenty-four Caprices, Op. 1: No. 24

1. Write a sentence to describe the rhythm of the theme.

2. Listen for examples of the following and, in each case, identify one or more variation in which it is to be found:

   (a) double stopping
   (b) chromatic scale
   (c) triplets
   (d) pizzicato
   (e) arpeggios
   (f) semiquavers

3. Name TWO ways in which Paganini makes the finale exciting.

Rondo

Vivaldi: *The Four Seasons* ('Autumn', movement III)

1. Name ONE instrument which plays the continuo part.

2. Choose TWO terms from the following list to describe the main rondo theme.

> in triple time   dissonant   uses a dotted rhythm
> chromatic   scalic   in quadruple time

3. Which of the following statements is true:

> **A** The rondo theme opens with the interval of a 3rd.
> **B** The rondo theme opens with the interval of a 5th.
> **C** The rondo theme opens with the interval of an octave.

4. How many times does the main rondo theme appear in the extract that you are listening to?

5. Comment on Vivaldi's use of dynamics in this movement.

6. Do you think that this piece was written in:

> **A** the sixteenth century
> **B** the eighteenth century
> **C** the nineteenth century

Weber: Clarinet Quintet in B♭ (movement IV)

1. Which of the following is the rhythm of the accompaniment in the first two bars?

2. Here is a plan of the first four sections of this movement. Describe the rondo theme and the two episodes that you hear.

> **A** bars 1–10 | **B** bars 11–23 | **A** bars 24–31 | **C** bars 32–68

3. This movement is taken from a clarinet quintet. Name the instruments in this ensemble.

4. Chose THREE terms from the following list that could be used to describe the clarinet part in the coda (track 23, 5′20″):

> semiquaver triplets   tremolo   scalic
> dotted rhythm   trill   andante

5. Name an ornament that is used in this section.

Ternary Form

Handel: 'He was despised' from *Messiah*

1. What is ternary form?

2. What type of aria is this?

3. Which instruments play the continuo part?

4. Is the singer a treble, an alto or a soprano?

5. How is the middle section contrasted with the outer sections?

6. When the first section returns, is it changed in any way?

Mozart: Symphony No. 40 (movement III)

1. This movement is taken from Mozart's Symphony No. 40. What is a symphony?

2. Describe TWO ways in which the trio contrasts with the minuet.

3. Name the three woodwind instruments which are soloists in the trio.

4. Name the only brass instrument to be heard in this movement.

5. In many symphonies from this period, the 'minuet and trio' movement is graceful and light-hearted. Do you think that applies to this example or has Mozart done something different?

Tchaikovsky: *Dance of the Reed Pipes* from *The Nutcracker*

1. This movement is in 2/4. Write out the rhythm of the opening accompaniment.

2. What technique are the strings using at the beginning of the piece? Is it:

   A tremolando
   B col legno
   C pizzicato

3. Describe THREE ways in which contrast between the sections is achieved.

4. This piece is in 2/4. Describe the rhythm played by the trumpets during the middle section.

5. Identify one place in this movement where you hear a *rallentando*.

6. Name the percussion instrument that is played on the final chord of the piece.

Area of Study 2
Serialism

Webern: Variations for Piano, Op. 27 (movement II)

1. When do you think this piece was written:

    A the eighteenth century
    B the twentieth century
    C the nineteenth century

2. What is meant by the term 'atonality'?

3. One of the ways a note row can be manipulated is by turning it upside down (inversion). Name another way it can be used.

4. Describe Webern's use of dynamics in this piece.

5. Choose THREE words from the following list to describe the music.

economic	diatonic	dissonant
legato	concentrated	lyrical

Stravinsky: *Fanfare for a New Theatre*

1. How does the music suggest an important occasion?

2. All the material in this short piece is derived from a note row. What is a note row?

3. What are the main ways in which a note row can be transformed in serial music?

4. Which of the following statements about the opening bar is true:

    A The two trumpets play a 5th apart.
    B The two trumpets play an octave apart.
    C The two trumpets play in unison.

5. How would you describe the rhythm of this composition?

6. The note row begins on A♯. Write out the remaining eleven notes.

7. Which trumpet plays the note row first?

Minimalism

Riley: *In C*

1. As the title tells us, this composition is in C. Identify TWO bars in the score that suggest another key.

2. This piece can be played on any instruments. How would you describe the instrumental combination that you can hear?

3. Describe the ostinato line that is heard throughout.

4. How has the composer created the texture of this piece?

Reich: *Clapping Music*

1. How many people are clapping?

2. Which of the following rhythms is the piece based on?

3. In this piece one performer repeats the same bar throughout. The other uses the same material but shifts the emphasis of the first beat. What effect does this have?

Experimental Music

Cage: *Living Room Music* ('Story')

1. How many voices can you hear?

2. Describe any interesting or unusual vocal techniques you can hear.

3. Look at the score. What unusual features do you notice about the notation?

4. Why did Cage not use conventional staff notation?

Cardew: *Treatise* (pages 190–191: two recordings)

1. What is this type of notation usually called?

2. Make a comparison of the two performances. Then:

   (a) name TWO of the instruments used in each performance;
   (b) describe how the two groups interpret the thick black lines on Page 190; and
   (c) describe how the two groups interpret the numbers 3 and 10 on Page 191.

3. In what way is this music aleatoric?

4. Describe TWO examples of extended instrumental techniques. You may refer to either performance.

5. Choose one of the pages and describe what musical treatment the score suggests to *you*. Name the instruments that you would use.

Monk: 'Wa-lie-oh' from *Songs from the Hill*

1. Give an example of an extended vocal technique used in this song.

2. Describe the opening section, which is based on the word 'Wa-lie-oh'. Outline the musical treatment Monk gives to this word.

3. Compare this piece with 'Story' from John Cage's *Living Room Music*. Identify TWO differences and TWO similarities.

4. The composer of *Songs from the Hill*, Meredith Monk, is also a performer. How might that have affected the composing process?

5. How has Monk managed to vary her material, yet also give the piece unity?

Electronic Music

Bedford: *The Song of the White Horse* ('The Blowing Stone')

1. Using the score, describe how the synthesizer is used in this movement.

2. How would you describe the music that the brass section plays:

    A counterpoint using triplets – *forte*
    B chords using sextuplets – *pianissimo*
    C chords using sextuplets – *forte*

3. Describe TWO ways in which the echo unit is used in this music.

4. What does the use of electronics add to this piece?

Wishart: *Vox 5*

1. This piece used a Vocoder, which is a type of synthesizer. What is a synthesizer?

2. Describe TWO ways in which Wishart uses the Vocoder to transform the sound of the voice.

3. Choose a term from the following list to describe the dynamics of (a) the first 30 seconds and (b) the last 30 seconds of the piece:

    sforzando   *mezzo-forte*   *diminuendo*
    crescendo   *subito piano*   *fortissimo*

Bricheno: *Hyde Park*

1. Look at the photograph and note down TWO words to describe the mood it conveys. How does Bricheno create the mood of the photograph in his music?

2. The piece is based on the sound of one instrument. Name this instrument.

3. Identify TWO ways in which the sound of the instrument is manipulated.

4. This is a multitrack recording. What is a multitrack recording?

5. (a) Panning, (b) stereo reverb and (c) delay were used on each track. Explain what ONE of these terms means.

Area of Study 3
12-Bar Blues

Casey Bill: *WPA Blues*

1. *WPA Blues* is in A major. Which three chords are used?

2. These are the words for Verse 1. Identify the words on which the harmony changes.

> VERSE 1
>
> *Everybody's workin' in this town*
> *And it's worried me night and day*
> *Everybody's workin' in this town*
> *And it's worried me night and day*
> *It's that mean workin' crew*
> *That works for the WPA*

3. How are the words typical of early blues music?

4. Which of the following statements is true:

   A The bass plays mostly on the first and third beats of the bar.
   B The bass plays mostly on the first and second beats of the bar.
   C The bass plays mostly on the second and fourth beats of the bar.

Bill Thomas: *I know you lied*

1. Describe the harmonic structure of this song.

2. The bass-guitar line has the same two-bar rhythm throughout. Which of the following is it?

3. Describe the first lead-guitar solo (starting at 1′27″) in one or two sentences.

4. How many bars long is this guitar solo? Is it:

   A 24 bars long
   B 12 bars long
   C 18 bars long

5. Name TWO features you can hear that identify *WPA Blues* as an older song than *I know you lied*.

Reggae

Delroy Washington: *Freedom Fighters*

1. The bass guitar makes much use of a repeated pattern throughout the song. Which of the following is it?

2. The vocal line uses blue notes. What are 'blue notes'?

3. The form of this song is verse and chorus punctuated by a guitar solo. Where does the guitar solo appear?

4. Which of the following statements is true:

    A The four-bar chord progression remains unchanged throughout the song.
    B The verse and chorus use different chord progressions.
    C The same one-bar chord progression is used throughout the song.

5. Write a paragraph describing the origins and influences of reggae music.

6. What aspect(s) of the words to this song is (are) typical of reggae?

Sound Dimension: *Real Rock*

1. Name the brass instrument that you can hear.

2. Name a keyboard instrument that you can hear.

3. Which beats of the bar are accented by the drums?

4. The harmony is very simple, with a limited number of chords repeated throughout. Which of the following best describes what you can hear:

    A one chord repeated
    B two chords repeated
    C three chords repeated

Club Dance Remix

Rae & Christian: *Spellbound* (Mix 1: featuring Veba, vocal)

1. What is the form of this song?

2. Where in the music do you hear a flute break?

3. The bass and drums form the rhythmic foundation of this song. Both use tape loops. What is a tape loop?

Rae & Christian: *Spellbound* (Mix 2: remix dub)

4. This is another mix of *Spellbound*. What is a mix?

5. Write a sentence about the use of vocals in this remix.

6. In the context of Club Dance Remix, what is a 'sample'?

Rae & Christian: *Spellbound* (Mix 3: Old English remix by Andy Madhatter and Si Brad)

7. Indicate whether each of the following statements is TRUE or FALSE:

    A In Mix 1 all the parts use syncopation.
    B Mix 2 uses verse and chorus form.
    C Mix 2 uses more brass sounds.
    D Mix 3 has a funky feel.

8. Describe the percussion part in this remix.

9. Name THREE ways in which music technology is used in these recordings.

LTJ Bukem: *Cosmic Interlude*

1. The structure of this track could be described as a collage. What is a collage?

2. What instruments feature throughout most of this mix?

3. Which of the following is the bass line in the opening bars of *Cosmic Interlude*?

4. Name a keyboard instrument featured on this track.

5. Do you think the mood of this music reflects the title?

Songs from Musicals

Bart: 'Consider Yourself' from *'Oliver!'*

1. What is a musical?

2. Which of the following is true of the time signature:

   A It is 6/8
   B It is 2/4
   C It is 4/4

3. Which verse also uses triple time?

4. There are four verses. For each verse indicate the number of voices singing, and name TWO distinctive musical features.

5. How does the music capture the bustle of the London streets?

Kander & Ebb: 'Cabaret' from *Cabaret*

1. Describe the eight-bar introduction to this song.

2. Listen to the first verse of the song. The singer's line is punctuated by chords. Which family of instruments plays these chords?

3. Indicate a place in the song where you hear:

   A an *accelerando*
   B a *rallentando*

4. Does the song stay in the same key throughout?

5. Where do you hear the highest note of the song?

6. How does the music reflect the words in this passage of the song?

   But when I saw her laid out like a queen,
   She was the happiest corpse I'd ever seen.
   I think of Elsie to this very day.
   I remember how she'd turn to me and say:
   What good is sitting alone in your room?
   Come hear the music play…

7. How is the excitement built up towards the end of the song?

Area of Study 4
Gamelan Music

Sekehe Gender Bharata Muni: *Langiang*

1. *Langiang* is used to accompany shadow puppet plays. What other roles does the gamelan perform in community life?

2. This piece is played by four metallophones. What is a metallophone and how is it played?

3. Describe the texture of *Langiang*.

4. *Langiang* uses slendro. What is 'slendro'?

5. What does gamelan notation look like? What purpose does it serve?

Gong Kebyar: *Jauk Masal*

1. What types of instruments can you hear playing?

2. Which two instruments play in the introduction?

3. Which instruments play the theme?

4. Which instruments punctuate the phrases of the theme?

5. *Jauk Masal* uses pelog. What is 'pelog'?

6. *Jauk Masal* is a Balinese masked dance depicting demons. Describe how the music conveys this.

7. How do we know that this music is coming to an end?

Indian Raga

Shruti Sadolikar Katkar: *Rag Durga*

1. Which instrument plays a drone in *Rag Durga*?

2. The singer is accompanied by a sarangi. Is this instrument bowed or plucked?

3. How many beats are there in the rhythm cycle played by the tabla:

    A 16   **B** 14   **C** 10

4. What is the name for this rhythmic cycle?

5. How are tabla played?

6. In Indian music, what is $S\ R\ G\ M\ P\ D\ N\ S$ an abbreviation for?

Buddhadev DasGupta: *Rag Brindabani Sarang*

1. What is a raga?

2. Name the first instrument that you hear playing, and describe its role in the music.

3. The first section of this piece lasts approximately one minute. What is the name for the opening section of a raga?

4. The soloist is playing a sarod. Describe a sarod.

5. What musical devices are used to make the music more exciting?

African Drumming

Drummers of Ghana: *Kundum*

1. Name TWO characteristic features of African drumming.

2. What is meant by 'call and response'?

3. What is a time-line?

4. What type of instrument plays the time-line in this piece?

5. After the introduction, one of the drums plays the same rhythm throughout Slow Kundum. Which of the following is it?

6. What is the role of the master drummer?

7. This piece of music, *Kundum*, is from Ghana. The Kundum festival celebrates the harvest of the Ahanta people who live in an area along the coast of Ghana. Write a paragraph describing other ways in which drums are part of musical life in Africa.

Les Percussions de Guinée: *Nzekele*

1. Describe how the arrival of the faster second section (which begins at 1′30″) is announced.

2. The piece opens with a flamboyant solo. What purpose do you think this solo serves?

3. How many different pitches does the lowest-sounding drum play?

4. Name TWO types of African drum.

5. What is a drum cue?

Music Drawing on Different Cultures

Harrison: Suite for Violin, Piano and Small Orchestra (Second Gamelan)

1. At the start there are two bars of 4/4 before the solo piano comes in. The harp repeats the same two-minim pattern. What is the interval between the minims:

    A a 5th
    B an octave
    C a 3rd

2. The tack piano and the celesta have the same rhythm in the opening. Is it:

    A continuous semiquavers
    B continuous quavers
    C continuous crotchets

3. How does Lou Harrison use his chosen instruments to resemble the sound of a gamelan?

4. Would you describe the music as consonant or dissonant? Give a reason why.

5. Compare this piece by Lou Harrison with either *Jauk Masal* or *Langiang*. Identify TWO differences and TWO similarities.

Labh Janjua & Panjabi MC: *Mundian To Bach Ke*

1. This is a bhangra song. What is 'bhangra' and where does it come from?

2. On what occasions would you normally hear bhangra played?

3. Describe the introduction, mentioning the instruments that you can hear playing.

4. This song uses a sample of the theme from *Knightrider*. What is a 'sample'?

5. The track uses elements from both Asia and the West. Give TWO examples of each.

6. The song has a simple form. Which of the following statements best describes it:

    A verse and chorus
    B 12-bar blues
    C verse and chorus with an introduction and a coda

7. Like many songs, this uses a bridge passage. What is a 'bridge passage'?

8. Towards the end of the song a scratch technique is used. What is 'scratching'?

Copyright Acknowledgements

Martland: Re-mix
© Copyright 1988 Schott & Co Limited, London
Reproduced by permission

Webern: Variations for Piano, Op.27
© Copyright 1937, 1979 Universal Edition A.G., Wien
Reproduced by permission

Stravinsky: Fanfare for a New Theatre
© Copyright 1968 Boosey & Hawkes Music Publishers Limited
Reproduced by permission of Boosey & Hawkes Music Publishers Limited

Riley: In C
© Copyright 1964 Ancient Word Music
Administered by Celestial Harmonies (BMI) and Temple Music (UK)
Reproduced by permission of Temple Music

Reich: Clapping Music
© Copyright 1980 Universal Edition (London) Limited, London
Reproduced by permission

Cage: Living Room Music
© Copyright 1976 Henmar Press Inc, New York
Reproduced by permission of Peters Edition Limited, London

Cardew: Treatise
© Copyright 1967 Gallery Upstairs Press, USA.
© Copyright 1970 assigned to Hinrichsen Edition, Peters Edition Limited, London. Reproduced by permission

Monk: Wa-lie-oh
© Copyright Meredith Monk
Reproduced by permission of Meredith Monk

Bedford: The Song of the White Horse
© Copyright 1977 Universal Edition (London) Limited, London
Reproduced by permission

Wishart: Vox 5
© Copyright Trevor Wishart. Reproduced by permission

Bricheno: Hyde Park
© Copyright Toby Bricheno. Reproduced by permission
Photograph: Hyde Park Subway © Copyright 2001 Sheila Brannigan

WPA Blues
Words & Music by William Weldon & Lester Melrose
© Copyright 1936 Universal/MCA Music Publishing Limited, 77 Fulham Palace Road, London. Used by permission of Music Sales Limited. All Rights Reserved. International Copyright Secured

Bill Thomas: I know you lied
© Copyright Bill Thomas. Reproduced by permission

Delroy Washington: Freedom Fighters
Words and Music by Delroy Washington
© Copyright 1976 EMI Virgin Music Limited, London WC2H 0QY
Reproduced by permission of International Music Publications Limited. All Rights Reserved

Dodd: Real Rock
© Copyright Jamrec Music
Reproduced by permission of Jamaica Recording and Publishing Studio Limited, Kingston, Jamaica, West Indies

Rae & Christian: Spellbound
Words and Music by David Pomeranz, Mark Rae, Steve Christian and Beverley Green
© Copyright 1998 Sony Music Publishing/Sony/ATV Music Publishing Ltd (90%) and Upward Spiral Music and Grand Central Music, USA (10%) Warner/Chappell Music Limited, London. Reproduced by permission of Sony Music Publishing Limited and International Music Publications Limited. All Rights Reserved

Cosmic Interlude
Music by Daniel Williamson
© Copyright 1998 Good Looking Music Limited, Warner/Chappell Music Limited, London W6 8BS. Reproduced by permission of International Music Publications Limited. All Rights Reserved

Consider Yourself
Words & Music by Lionel Bart
© Copyright 1959 Lakeview Music Publishing Company Limited, Universal Music Publishing, 77 Fulham Palace Road, London. Used by permission of Music Sales Limited. All Rights Reserved. International Copyright Secured

Cabaret
Words by Fred Ebb. Music by John Kander
© Copyright 1966 Times Square Music Publications, USA Carlin Music Corp, London NW1 8BD. Reproduced by permission of International Music Publications Limited. All Rights Reserved

Langiang
Published by EMI Music / Silva Screen Music Publishers. Reproduced by permission

Kundum
Reproduced by permission of HoneyRock, 396 Raystown Road, Everett, PA 15537, USA

Lou Harrison: Suite for Violin, Piano and Small Orchestra
© Copyright 1985 C F Peters Corporation, New York
Reproduced by permission of Peters Edition Limited, London

Labh Janjua & Panjabi MC: Mundian To Bach Ke
Reproduced by permission of Nachural

Although every effort has been made to trace and acknowledge all copyright material, the Publishers will be grateful for information in order to rectify any omissions

Index

A

'Autumn' from *The Four Seasons* (Vivaldi) · 34

B

Bali:
    Jauk Masal · 120
    Langiang · 119
Bart, Lionel: *'Consider Yourself'* from *'Oliver!'* · 104
Bedford, David: *The Song of the White Horse* (*'The Blowing Stone'*) · 86
Beethoven, Ludwig van: *Thirty-three Variations on a Waltz by Diabelli (theme and variations 1–4)* · 25
Bhangra: *Mundian To Bach Ke* · 136
'Blowing Stone, The' (Bedford) · 86
Blues, *WPA* (Weldon and Melrose) · 92
Bricheno, Toby: *Hyde Park* · 90
Buddhadev DasGupta: *Rag Brindabani Sarang* · 123
Bukem, LTJ: *Cosmic Interlude* · 103

C

Cabaret (Kander & Ebb) · 108
Cage, John: *Living Room Music* (*'Story'*) · 74
Caprice, Op. 1: No. 24 (Paganini) · 30
Cardew, Cornelius: *Treatise (pages 190–191)* · 80
Casey Bill (Weldon): *WPA Blues* · 92
Clapping Music (Reich) · 73
Clarinet Quintet in B♭ (Weber) · 40
'Consider Yourself' (Bart) · 104
Cosmic Interlude (LTJ Bukem) · 103

D

Dance of the Reed Pipes (Tchaikovsky) · 61
'Diabelli' Variations (Beethoven) · 25

F

Fanfare for a New Theatre (Stravinsky) · 70
Freedom Fighters (Delroy Washington) · 96

G

Gamelan (No. 2) from *Suite for Violin, Piano and Small Orchestra* (Harrison) · 133
Ghana: *Kundum* · 124

Gong Kebyar, Sebatu: *Jauk Masal* · 120
Guinea: *Nzekele* · 126

H

Handel, George Frideric: *'He was despised'* from *Messiah* · 52
Harrison, Lou: *Suite for Violin, Piano and Small Orchestra (Second Gamelan)* · 133
'He was despised' (Handel) · 52
'Here the deities approve' (Purcell) · 9
Hyde Park (Bricheno) · 90

I

I know you lied (Bill Thomas) · 94
In C (Riley) · 71
India:
    Rag Brindabani Sarang · 123
    Rag Durga · 122

J

Jauk Masal (Bali) · 120

K

Kander & Ebb: *'Cabaret'* from *Cabaret* · 108
Kundum (Ghana) · 124

L

Langiang (Bali) · 119
Les Percussions de Guinée: *Nzekele* · 126
Living Room Music (Cage) · 74
LTJ Bukem: *Cosmic Interlude* · 103

M

Marais, Marin: *Sonnerie de Ste Geneviève du mont de Paris* · 13
Martland, Steve: *Re-mix* · 24
Messiah (Handel) · 52
Minuet and trio from *Symphony No. 40 in G minor* (Mozart) · 56
Monk, Meredith: *'Wa-lie-oh'* from *Songs from the Hill* · 83
Mozart, Wolfgang Amadeus: *Symphony No. 40 in G minor (movement III)* · 56
Mundian To Bach Ke (Panjabi MC) · 136

N

Nutcracker, The (Tchaikovsky) · 61
Nzekele (Guinea) · 126

O

'Oliver!' (Bart) · 104

P

Paganini, Nicolò: *Twenty-four Caprices,*
   Op. 1: No. 24 · 30
Panjabi MC: *Mundian To Bach Ke* · 136
Purcell, Henry: *'Here the deities approve'*
   from *Welcome to all the Pleasures* · 9

Q

Quintet in B♭ for Clarinet and Strings (Weber) · 40

R

Rae & Christian:
   Spellbound (Mix 1) featuring Veba (vocals) · 99
   Spellbound (Mix 2) remix dub · 101
   Spellbound (Mix 3) Old English remix
      (Madhatter & Brad) · 102
Rag Brindabani Sarang (India) · 123
Rag Durga (India) · 122
Real Rock (Sound Dimension) · 98
Reich, Steve: *Clapping Music* · 73
Re-mix (Martland) · 24
Riley, Terry: *In C* · 71

S

Sekehe Gender Bharata Muni: *Langiang* · 119
Shruti Sadolikar Katkar: *Rag Durga* · 122
Song of the White Horse, The (Bedford) · 86
Songs from the Hill (Monk) · 83
Sonnerie de Ste Geneviève du mont de Paris
   (Marais) · 13
Sound Dimension: *Real Rock* · 98

Spellbound
   (Mix 1) featuring Veba (vocals)
      (Rae & Christian) · 99
   (Mix 2) remix dub (Rae & Christian) · 101
   (Mix 3) Old English remix (Rae & Christian/
      Madhatter & Brad) · 102
'Story' (Cage) · 74
Stravinsky, Igor: *Fanfare for a New Theatre* · 70
Suite for Violin, Piano and Small Orchestra
   (Harrison) · 133
Symphony No. 40 in G minor (Mozart) · 56

T

Tchaikovsky, Pyotr: *Dance of the Reed Pipes*
   from *The Nutcracker* · 61
The Four Seasons (Vivaldi) · 34
Thirty-three Variations on a Waltz by Diabelli
   (Beethoven) · 25
Thomas, Bill: *I know you lied* · 94
Treatise (Cardew) · 80
Twenty-four Caprices, Op. 1 (Paganini) · 30

V

Variations for Piano, Op. 27 (Webern) · 69
Vivaldi, Antonio: *The Four Seasons*
   ('Autumn', movement III) · 34
Vox 5 (Wishart) · 89

W

'Wa-lie-oh' (Monk) · 83
Washington, Delroy: *Freedom Fighters* · 96
Weber, Carl Maria von: *Clarinet Quintet in B♭*
   (movement IV) · 40
Webern, Anton: *Variations for Piano, Op. 27*
   (movement II) · 69
Welcome to all the Pleasures (Purcell) · 9
Weldon, Casey Bill: *WPA Blues* · 92
Wishart, Trevor: *Vox 5* · 89
WPA Blues (Weldon & Melrose) · 92

The New Anthology of Music
Edited by Julia Winterson

The New Anthology of Music
- Book   EP 7591   ISBN 1-901507-03-3
- Set of 4 CDs   EP 7591cd   ISBN 1-901507-04-1

THE NEW ANTHOLOGY OF MUSIC is an exciting collection of more than sixty pieces of music, each with a recording and a transcription. From Dowland to Reich, string quartet to steel band, raga to reggae, the New Anthology covers a wide range of music: classical, world, popular and jazz. This comprehensive publication is designed to accompany the Advanced Subsidiary and Advanced GCE in Music and will also be a useful resource for GCSE teachers and anyone who wishes to learn more about music. The book and four-CD set cover nine Areas of Study: Music for Large Ensemble, 20th-Century Art Music, Music for Small Ensemble, Keyboard Music, Sacred Vocal Music, Secular Vocal Music, Music for Film and Television, Popular Music and Jazz, and World Music.
Prepared for publication by Peter Nickol

- For:
  Edexcel Advanced Subsidiary GCE in Music
  Edexcel Advanced GCE in Music
- Containing more than 60 pieces in printed score
- With a 4-CD pack of recorded performances
- Covering 9 Areas of Study

Contents:

Keyboard Music
Sweelinck	Pavana Lachrimae
J. S. Bach	Partita No. 4 in D major, BWV 828: Sarabande and Gigue
Mozart	Piano Sonata in B♭ K333: Movement I
Schumann	Kinderscenen, Op. 15: Nos. 1, 3 and 11
Debussy	Pour le piano: Sarabande
Shostakovich	Prelude and Fugue in A Op. 87 No. 7

Music For Small Ensemble
Holborne	Pavane 'The image of melancholy' and Galliard 'Ecce quam bonum'
G. Gabrieli	Sonata pian' e forte
Corelli	Trio sonata in D Op. 3 No. 2: Movement IV
Haydn	String quartet in E♭ Op. 33 No. 2 'The Joke': Movement IV
Beethoven	Septet in E♭ Op. 20: Movement I
Brahms	Piano quintet in F minor: Movement III
Poulenc	Sonata for Horn, Trumpet and Trombone: Movement I

Music for Large Ensemble
J. S. Bach	Brandenburg Concerto No. 4 in G: Movement I
Haydn	Symphony No. 26 in D minor 'Lamentatione': Movement I
Berlioz	Harold in Italy: Movement III
Wagner	Tristan und Isolde: Prelude
Debussy	Prélude à l'après-midi d'un faune
Tippett	Concerto for Double String Orchestra: Movement I

Sacred Vocal Music
Taverner	O Wilhelme, pastor bone
Gabrieli	In ecclesiis
J. S. Bach	Cantata No. 48 'Ich elender Mensch': Movements 1–4
Haydn	Nelson Mass: Quoniam tu solus sanctus
Bruckner	Locus iste
Stravinsky	Symphony of Psalms: Movement III
Tavener	The Lamb

Secular Vocal Music
Dowland	Flow my tears
Weelkes	Sing we at pleasure
Monteverdi	Ohimè, se tanto amate
Purcell	Dido and Aeneas: Thy hand, Belinda – When I am laid in earth
Haydn	My mother bids me bind my hair
Schubert	Der Doppelgänger
Fauré	Après un rêve
Schoenberg	Pierrot Lunaire: Der kranke Mond
Gershwin	Porgy and Bess: Summertime

20th Century Art Music
Stravinsky	Pulcinella: Sinfonia, Gavotta and Vivo
Webern	Quartet Op. 22: Movement I
Shostakovich	String Quartet No. 8 Op.110: Movement I
Cage	Sonatas and Interludes for Prepared Piano: Sonatas I–III
Berio	Sequenza III for Female Voice
Reich	New York Counterpoint: Movement II

Television and Film Music
Auric	Passport to Pimlico
Bernstein	On the Waterfront
Goldsmith	Planet of the Apes
Williams	ET
Pheloung	Inspector Morse
Horner	Titanic

World Music
Ram Narayan	Rag Bhairav
Gong Kebyar de Sebatu	Baris Melamphahan
Red Stripe Ebony Steelband	Yellow Bird
Niall Keegan	Tom McElvogue's Jig; New Irish Barndance
Mustapha Tettey Addy	Agbekor Dance
Familia Valera Miranda	Se quema la chumbamba

Popular Music and Jazz
Louis Armstrong	West End Blues
Duke Ellington	Black and Tan Fantasie
Miles Davis	Four
Howlin' Wolf	I'm leavin' you
Carl Perkins	Honey don't
Kinks	Waterloo Sunset
Beatles	A day in the life*
Desmond Dekker	You can get it if you really want
Van Morrison	Tupelo honey
Oasis	Don't look back in anger

* Not included on CD

Edexcel
Success through qualifications